CONTENTS

First Week: Francis and the Living Nativity   5

    Introduction   5
    First Sunday of Advent   7
    First Week Meditations: Days One through Five   9
    Weekend Activity   23

Second Week: From the Second Manger
to Contemporary Expression   25

    Introduction   25
    Second Sunday of Advent   26
    Second Week Meditations: Days One through Five   28
    Weekend Activity   41

Third Week: The Living Nativity in Global and
Personal Context   43

    Introduction   43
    Third Sunday of Advent   44
    Third Week Meditations: Days One through Five   46
    Weekend Activity   60

Fourth Week: Heightened Anticipation   63

Introduction   63
Fourth Sunday of Advent   64
Fourth Week Meditations: Days One through Five   66
Weekend Activity   77

Fifth Week: Challenges and Resolutions   79

Introduction   79
First Sunday after Christmas   80
Fifth Week Meditations: Days One through Six   82
Weekend Activity   95
Epiphany   95

Leader's Guide   99

First Week Group Meeting   100
Second Week Group Meeting   103
Third Week Group Meeting   105
Fourth Week Group Meeting   107
Fifth Week Group Meeting   108

Notes   111

About the Author   112

Francis and the Living Nativity

Introduction

Saint Francis, in the thirteenth century, is credited with creating the first living nativity, a reenactment of the birth of Jesus in a Bethlehem stable. I like to think of Saint Francis creating this second manger in a cave with hay and animals so that we would know the humbleness of the first manger and the Child who enters into the ordinary, common, and simple world of humanity.

We will use the life of Saint Francis as a lens to explore the beginnings and variety of nativity and Advent traditions and the centrality of the Incarnation, not only for Saint Francis, but also for people today looking for signs of God's love. We will look at the ordinary ways and common traditions used to prepare for the birth of the Christ child.

As our journey to Christmas begins, I invite you to pray this prayer. Feel free to add your own thoughts.

Holy One, into such a world as ours and such a time as this, you chose to enter. Again and again, you visit us in the darkest times of life. Again and again, you surprise us in the midst of hectic schedules, tense cities, world crises, and worried lives.

Loving God, help us keep alert in this Advent season. Help us to slow down for prayer, to stand up for justice, to breathe deeply your love each day. Open us and make us ready for you. Amen.

You may read this book individually, with your family, or with a group that gathers weekly to discuss it and pray together.

Each week, there is a reading for every weekday of Advent, something to ponder and reflect upon, and a time of prayer. The sixth day suggests a weekend activity. I encourage you to make notes as you reflect and refer to them if you gather for a discussion with others on each of the four Sundays of Advent. Each Sunday includes a reading, prayers, and a ritual for lighting Advent candles on an Advent wreath. There is a fifth week of meditations with a focus on New Year's Day and Epiphany.

There is also a small-group guide at the end of the book that gives fuller instructions for a weekly mini retreat, a bit longer time for a group to share and participate in a suggested group activity. If you are part of a group, look at the small-group guide to see the order of the meeting and the activities suggested.

If possible, make an Advent wreath for you and your home. Include any family or friends who might be joining you in the evenings (or other designated time) for the ritual of prayer and candle lighting. An Advent wreath can be any circular base that holds four candles, preferably purple or blue. Some stores sell an Advent candle set that includes three purple or blue candles and a pink candle, which is traditionally lit on the third Sunday of Advent.

Some traditions also include a white candle in the center to represent the Christ child, which is lit on Christmas Eve or Day.

Clay, wood, or other materials provide creative wreath-making options. Styrofoam (while not so earth friendly) purchased at craft stores works well for families with small children who want to help by adding pine branches to cover the wreath base. Many religious stores or online sites sell Advent wreaths of brass or pottery that you may use every year. Find or make a wreath that works for you and keep it on the table where you dine or in another prominent place for the Advent and Christmas season.

Each day, light a candle as you enter the time of prayer.

God's blessings as you begin your Advent journey.

First Sunday of Advent

We do not know exactly when the tradition of celebrating the four weeks and Sundays that we call Advent began. While the feast of Christmas was observed by the fourth century, it is not until the later part of the sixth century that we have record of homilies for particular Sundays in Advent, which indicates that the practice of preparing for Christmas was numbered and named as Advent. Evidently, some parts of Europe had five Sundays of Advent, but documents show that Pope Gregory VII changed the number to four in the eleventh century. Today, we carry on the tradition of preparing for Christmas with four Sundays and their weekdays. Likewise, we observe the tradition of preparing for the other great Christian celebration, Easter, with the fifty-day journey of Lent.

As you pray, please change the personal pronouns as needed to make the prayers speak to you. The prayers are written with the thought that even as we pray alone, we participate in a whole world of prayer going on at all times, in all places, and all around us.

Centering Time

Take a few deep breaths. Breathe in peace with each inhale. Breathe out worry with each exhale. Breathe in peace, let go of anxiety.

Pray

Cause us to breathe deeply, Loving God, just for this moment, a letting go of worry and anxiety about all that's left to do. Center us in your amazing grace so that we may hear the flutter of angel wings, know the gift of your peace, receive the gift of our healing, and live in the grace of your forgiveness.

May each breath open us to the simple and beautiful ways you are with us. Open us to the Child who comes to love us. Amen.

Reading

Choose from Jeremiah 33:14-16; Psalm 25:1-10; or Luke 21: 34-36.

These are lessons often read for the first Sunday of Advent. They may have been used in a worship service that you attended today. You may wish to explore the readings using different translations and having different readers. You may also choose different readings from your faith community.

Candle Lighting

Light one candle on the Advent wreath.

Prayer: *One candle can chase away the darkness. May this candle shine bright this night (or day), O God, and lead us to a deep place, a holy space where we discover an incredible love, your love shining to us from a manger. Help us see, really see, how much you love us and go with us through each day.*

You may light the candle each evening before the meditation or when you pray.

Prayers

Lift up any joys or concerns in a time of prayer.

One pattern of sharing encourages the person praying to say, "This is my prayer" after mentioning an intention for a person or situation. Others then may respond, "This is our prayer."

Use this pattern or discover a pattern that works for you.

A Look Ahead

Before concluding your prayers around the Advent wreath, think about your coming week. Notice any events, meetings, or activities that you may want to hold in prayer as part of your daily reading and reflection.

Day One

Desire and Fervor

Our introduction to the Advent season and our lens for seeing the breadth of Christmas traditions comes from the thirteenth-century life of Saint Francis. He was born in 1181/82 to a well-to-do family in Assisi, Italy, baptized Giovanni de Pietro di Bernadone, but was generally known as Francesco. He enjoyed a good life in the prosperous home of a cloth merchant, was well-liked, and was popular at parties. He tried on the assumed glorious life of soldier, but was captured, imprisoned, and held for ransom. After a year in prison, he returned home ill but still seeking some higher or better glory. He thought joining soldiers of the Fourth Crusade might lead to returning as a prince, but a powerful dream turned him around before any battle occurred, much to the disappointment of his father, who had outfitted his son with horse and armor. Francis entered into a period of prayer and confession. A chance encounter with a leper and a mystical experience where he heard God telling him to "go repair my house which is falling into ruins," turned his life toward compassion for all—especially for the poor—and gave him a purpose and a mission.

Francis started to rebuild the church at San Damiano, just outside the walled city of Assisi, while continuing his spiritual journey by adopting simplicity and poverty as his companions. He discovered newfound compassion for all creation—for the forgotten of his society—and he began to preach of God's love and peace. His joy in life and in following Jesus attracted others to him, which led to developing a rule or guide for living for his followers.

The stories about Francis are many and inspiring. I will share some of them in these pages but the primary one for Advent is his creation of the Christmas crèche.

The earliest biography of Francis was written by Thomas of Celano in 1228. Thomas knew Francis and was one of his followers, though he was not one of his earliest disciples. Thomas was commissioned by Pope Gregory IX to write the biography in the year that Francis was canonized and henceforth became, Saint Francis. In thirty chapters, he tells many stories of Saint Francis, including the first outdoor nativity celebration.

In the chapter recounting the living nativity at Greccio, Italy, he begins with a passionate description of Saint Francis. "His highest aim, foremost desire, and greatest intention was to pay heed to the holy gospel in all things and through all things, to follow the teaching of our Lord Jesus Christ and to retrace his footsteps completely with all vigilance and all zeal, all the desire of his soul and all the fervor of his heart."[1]

The extroverted, good-times fellow became a passionate, enthusiastic follower of Jesus. Francis was no half-hearted, lukewarm, casual, tepid, or fair-weather disciple. He made following Jesus his "highest aim" with "all the desire of his soul." He was consumed with the words and teaching of Jesus.

Thomas continues, "So thoroughly did the humility of the Incarnation and the charity of the Passion occupy his memory that he scarcely wanted to think of anything else."[2] Francis wanted everyone to see, in their own time and place, what the love of God looks like and the extent to which God would bend to restore human dignity. The love of God, for Francis, looked like a baby.

Many of us live distracted lives, constantly pulled in many directions and interrupted by phone calls, texts, crying babies, sirens, and children's schedules. It is hard to imagine being so focused on any one thing that we would use the superlatives that Thomas uses to describe Saint Francis.

One contemporary author, Cal Newport, has written a book about our distracted world and the need for what he calls *deep work*. *Deep work* is the clearing away of cell phones, emails, and texts so that one may focus on one task with clarity, abundant time, and even solitude. He tells one story about a businessperson who paid for a long trip to the far east so that he would have the whole plane ride over and back to think about a big project without common distractions.

As we enter these four weeks of preparation, I invite you to look for and plan for times of quiet reflection with this book and with the contemplation of the Loving God who chooses to come and dwell with us in the life of Jesus.

This week's Psalm reminds us to put our trust in God (Ps. 25:2) and pray that God would show us the way and teach us the right paths to follow (v. 4). We are on the path to Bethlehem, mindful of distractions, but with Saint Francis and scripture to guide us.

Ponder

What is your greatest zeal? What would your family or friends say you are most passionate about?

How do you deal with distractions during your day? How would you carve out a sustained period of solitude, either to spend in prayer or to focus on a big project, a big idea, or a major transition?

Light one candle on your wreath if you did not do so earlier. Choose your own time for lighting your candle each evening.

Pray

Let this be your prayer or a starter for your own words.

> Something stirs deep within
>   a memory of a distant harmony
>   a longing for connection
>   a feeling of warmth.
>
> Stirred by the twinkling of light
>   the gathering of friends
>   the clear, still, and holy night.
>
> Something stirs deep within
>   a simple story about a baby
>   a shaking of assumptions and fears
>   and a God who bends low to be with us.

Day Two

Preparation

In Greccio, Italy, there lived a nobleman of good reputation and exemplary spiritual life by the name of John. Despite his place as "nobility," Francis had a special affection for John and used his cave as a place for prayer whenever he visited. According to Thomas of Celano, as Francis developed this idea of a celebration of the Nativity, he called John and said, "Hurry before me and carefully make ready the things I tell you. For I wish to enact the memory of that Babe who was born in Bethlehem: to see as much as is possible with my own bodily eyes the discomfort of his infant needs, how he lay in a manger, and how, with an ox and an ass standing by, he rested on hay."[3]

I like knowing that this exchange happened some fifteen days before Christmas. It takes time to get our souls, our churches, our houses, and ourselves ready for a major celebration. It takes attention to detail if we intend to gather the elements that will call to mind the first Nativity.

For my family, preparation touches many parts of our house. On the outside of the house, I hang white Christmas lights. Each house we have lived in received a different arrangement depending on the house and landscape. I use white lights because there is a good chance they will be up a long time, especially in those snowy places we have lived where I didn't want to brave the snow and cold to climb ladders in January. The white lights in February or March can light the way for visitors or cheer us up on a dark evening.

We have a set of Christmas dishes and mugs, so we change out the everyday dishes for these special seasonal ones. We still use place mats that the children made out of old Christmas cards placed on poster board and covered with clear contact paper. In the center of the table is a pottery Advent wreath.

Pictures of the Nativity replace several of the pictures hanging on our walls. One is a needlepoint that my sister made several years ago. One is made of colors, glue, and glitter that depicts a cheerful manger scene created by our young son. Three are a signed set by the contemporary artist John August Swanson, portraying the shepherds, the birth, and the magi.

Usually we make a pilgrimage to a Christmas tree farm to cut down a tree. Most of the decorations on the tree have a story or a history, so decorating can take a long time if we tell all the stories. But the memories of each ornament are precious.

We bring out the Advent and Christmas CDs and tapes. (Yes, we still have some cassette tapes.) Music plays while we decorate the house and continues most mornings in Advent while we eat breakfast—good balance as I read the news of the world.

We put the box of Christmas books on a shelf. We used to read them with our young children, but now I find myself using the picture books for adult retreats that I lead. There is something special about sitting in front of a fireplace and enjoying a wonderful children's story while on a retreat.

And there are the nativity sets. We clear all shelves and flat spaces of pictures, plants, etc. to make room for the eighty crèches. As we recently moved, we had to discover all new places for the nativities. We have our favorite sets, and they get prime locations. We place a small card with the name of the country or origin by the sets and add cards for the new ones we receive whenever one of the family or a friend travels to a new country.

At the churches I served, there were Advent and Christmas preparations. Altar cloths were changed to purple or blue and new banners were hung—some made by the children. A large Advent wreath was prepared for the sanctuary and, often on the first Sunday, we had a wreath-making table after worship so families could make and take their own table centerpiece.

Back to Assisi: "Once the good and faithful man (John) had heard Francis's words, he ran quickly and prepared in that place all the things that the holy man had requested."[4] Intended or not, the whole description of Francis's request and John's response reminds me of Jesus' instructions to his disciples in preparing for the Palm Sunday ride into Jerusalem (Luke 19:30-38) and the preparation for the Passover meal (Luke 22:8-13). Francis felt the same urgency as we sense in the Gospels to prepare for the Babe of Bethlehem to come alive in a new way for his friars (the men who committed to following Francis) and the people. Thus, we too prepare to experience again the mystery and wonder of God with us.

Ponder

How do you prepare your house for Advent or Christmas? How does your faith community prepare?

What is a favorite children's book to read again? Or a new one from the library or a bookstore?

How do you prepare yourself to kneel at Bethlehem?

Light one candle on your wreath.

Pray

Pray this prayer or let it be a starter for your own words.

Holy Child, Loving Savior, we sense the coming of your birth. We feel the creeping hustle and bustle that pushes you to the side. We feel the burden of lists and obligations that drain our joy and dull our spirit. We see the flurry of holiday bargains that know not of the holy day that is to come. So we hear your words to keep awake, we watch so we will see you and know your presence in our lives. Come and open our hearts to the unexpected moments of joy. Come and light your candles of peace in our troubled world. Come and set your place at our tables. We are ready. Amen.

Day Three

Celebration

Thomas of Celano turns into a poet when he describes Francis and that Christmas Eve service outside a cave in Greccio. As he oversees preparation of the manger, the hay placed, and the animals brought in, it is clear that "the time of exultation has come . . . the night is lit up like day, delighting both man and beast. The people arrive, ecstatic at this new mystery of new joy. The forest amplifies the cries and the boulders echo back the joyful crowd."[5]

As in the Holy Week entry into Jerusalem (Luke 19:40), even the rocks and boulders have a place in the story of God's presence with humanity. All creation takes part in the unfolding of God's love in Jesus as Saint Francis brings the story to life.

"The holy man of God stands before the manger, filled with heartfelt sighs, contrite in his piety, and overcome with wondrous joy."[6] Sometimes it is the simplest of things that causes a catch in our breath or tears in the corners of our eyes: wondrous joy that takes away our words, a moment of awe that stops us in our tracks, a deep sigh that slows us down and eases us into reverence.

"There simplicity is given a place of honor, poverty is exalted, humility is commended, and out of Greccio is made a new Bethlehem."[7]

The words of Thomas create pictures in my mind of a night of wonder and joy and community and holiness. People experienced a new Bethlehem moment in all its simplicity, poverty, and humility—hallmarks of the first Nativity and guiding practices for the brothers and others who followed Francis and the way he followed Jesus.

I believe that many who come to a Christmas Eve service are hoping for their own Bethlehem moment, an affirmation of God's presence, a glimpse of lasting joy, a time of healing or forgiveness. Those are heavy expectations to put on a worship service, but, with Francis as guide, with preparations made, and the simple enactment or telling of the story, people may catch a glimpse of joy, feel the lift of burdens, and the flood of peace. This experience can happen whether our services are more elaborate with a brass ensemble and full choir or a children's pageant with bathrobes and wire wings. Bethlehem moments can happen anywhere.

One time I visited the religious community called Taizé in France. Many know of it because of its music and its commitment to serve the needy. Taizé attracts thousands of young people every summer who travel there to study, worship, and pray. I arrived by bus late one night and walked up the hill to the town. It was mostly dark, and I was not sure where to go. I heard music and followed the sound to a building. I opened the door to dim light that revealed monks in white robes, many candles, and such beautiful singing. My pack slid off my shoulders and I knelt on the floor in amazement. It was a moment of peace and awe and, looking back, it was a Bethlehem moment of holiness.

As we get closer to Christmas, we will explore more ways of celebrating Bethlehem moments as individuals and as communities of faith.

Ponder

Can you name or describe any Bethlehem moments that you have experienced? Name a time when you felt God's presence and maybe even knelt like shepherds and magi.

Saint Francis intentionally chose the cave at Greccio. Is there a special place where you would choose to spend Christmas Eve or Christmas Day? What draws you to that place?

Light one candle on your wreath.

Pray

Loving God, deep in the night, when the entire world had locked the doors on love and closed the shutters on hope, you pierced the darkness with Light and a Baby's cry. Never again shall we be alone. No more shall we sit in fear. A wondrous joy permeates our world.

God of angels and babies, open us once again to this miracle, this wonder that you become one with us. Let the angels lead us in song. Let the stars shine every night until Christmas. Let our hearts be ready, ever ready. Amen.

Day Four

Preaching the Word

Francis preaches to the community gathered at Greccio. It is as if he sings the gospel. He "pours forth sweet honey about the birth of the poor King and the poor city of Bethlehem . . . he often calls Christ the 'Babe from Bethlehem' whenever he means to call him Jesus . . . He seems to lick his lips whenever he uses the expressions 'Jesus' or 'Babe from Bethlehem,' tasting the word on his happy palate and savoring the sweetness of the word."[8]

Evidently, Francis was a good preacher and communicator, with a powerful and clear voice, persuasively drawing people to him and the gospel. His life-of-the-party personality translated into a passionate and winsome spokesman for Jesus. He was alive with joy, and people caught the spirit and left with a new commitment to joy and to the "Babe of Bethlehem."

According to Thomas of Celano, the preaching and celebration helped multiply the gifts of God. One person had a vision during the service in which he saw a little child lying lifeless in the manger, and he saw Francis approach the child and waken him as if from a deep sleep.

Thomas interprets the vision as a commentary on the times with many people asleep to the Holy Child, to the presence of God in their lives. This Bethlehem moment shows that God is waking up individuals and the church through the holy man Francis. The Nativity carries a wake-up call and proclaims that God is present in the humble and poor places where many people find themselves.

One always hopes that preaching is alive and fresh and connects people to the living God, the loving Jesus, and the powerful Spirit; but I don't know many people who experience visions in our worship services. Yet, words are powerful and so is the setting and the designs for the worship experience. Words, music, silence, and visuals all come together to create a moment when we notice, feel, hear, and respond to God.

I spent a sabbatical year living in a Quaker community and discovered a different weaving of word and silence than I was used to. Out of the silence, sometimes a worshipper would speak, and often it was simple and profound. The silence surrounded the words, so they could be received and reflected upon. The Quakers also had a name for when God's Spirit was present and felt so palpably that often I would open my eyes to see what was there. They called this spiritual experience a "gathered" or "covered meeting." At these times, maybe some visions were occurring.

Ponder

Describe a worship experience or a sermon that touched you deeply, awakened you to the presence of God, and released you from wounds or hurts that blocked your growth.

What within you needs to be awakened and brought to new life?

Light one candle on your wreath.

Pray

Holy God, sing to us in the stillness of this moment. Speak to us in the depths of our hearts. Open our ears to hear the brush of angel wings and open our eyes to see miracles all around us.

Let there be a space for you in the midst of all the hurry and rush, a holy and inner place that cherishes silence and song and words spoken true. In our busy lives, may we keep a candle lit and a manger ready, at least in our hearts.

God of all time and seasons, create in us an open space for your birth. Amen.

Day Five

Miracles

The second manger and celebration ended but the story did not end. Again, Thomas of Celano describes happenings that would be unusual to us, surprising to many, and miracles to others. Thomas makes no judgment, but records that "it came to pass in the surrounding area that many of the animals, suffering from various diseases, were freed from their illness when they ate some of this hay [from the manger]. What is more, women who had been suffering with long and hard labor had an easy delivery after they placed some of this hay upon themselves. Finally, an entire group of people of both sexes obtained much desired relief from an assortment of afflictions."[9]

We may wonder at such stories about the saints, and Saint Francis certainly has his share of incredible moments and encounters; yet people in that day knew that things happened that had no rational explanation. In a pre-scientific time, objects had power and there was a reverence for items connected to a holy person or event. Today, we talk about the placebo effect and the importance of belief and trust in a doctor or procedure. Maybe the holy man of God, Francis, by his personality and joy, evoked a hope and belief that healing and change could happen through the holy manger.

God is a loving and supportive presence in the midst of illnesses and accidents, even if there are no surprises or unexpected changes that we call miracles. Often, we lean into science for answers to our questions. We perform tests to figure out what factors were involved in a surprising or unexpected change. But sometimes doctors and scientists and researchers have no logical or rational reason for the change or healing or different outcome. We may know of people whose cancer disappeared or shrank without the benefit of chemotherapy or surgery. Others have witnessed the healing of broken bones or have survived without any injuries from a fall off a high building. Flora Wuellner, in her book, *Miracle*, writes, "Sometimes, though, for reasons we do not completely understand, God's longing and power to heal pours through swiftly and fully, not waiting for the slow, groaning transformations of our choices or for the transition of nature itself."[10]

No matter what happens, there is still mystery to life and more that we do not understand. "We cannot put a miracle in a bottle and sell it."[11]

While I applaud and am grateful for the effort to know more, I think it is good to leave a little room for the mysterious. As Howard Thurman, Dean of the Chapel at Howard University and at Boston University wrote, "There must be always remaining in everyone's life some place for the singing of angels, some place for that which in itself is breathlessly beautiful and, by an inherent prerogative, throws all the rest of life into a new and creative relatedness. . . ."[12]

Ponder

Recall a story or incident in your own life where some healing or surprise came unexpectedly. How was prayer a part of the story? How did you give thanks?

What in your life is "breathlessly beautiful" and causes you to pause, celebrate, or kneel?

Light one candle on your wreath.

Pray

God comes to us, where we are—
in between darkness and light,
stuck with lists and burdened with tasks.
God comes to us, as we are—
anxious and worried,
hopeful and blessed.
God comes to us
as wisdom from afar,
as light in our darkness,
as surprise and miracle,
as hope for life eternal.
God comes to us, here and now.

Weekend Activity

This weekend might be a good time to visit a farm if one is near you. How are animals fed? What are the smells and sounds of a farm? Some farms in December have hayrides or sleigh rides drawn by horses. Can you arrange for some experience that connects you to farm animals that may have been at the "second manger?"

You may also wish to try your hand a building a manger. A large manger could be for outside as part of your Christmas home decorations. Or maybe a group from your faith community wishes to build a manger for the worship space or outside. Add some straw but don't put the baby Jesus in the manger yet. Are there any animals that you could add to the large nativity?

A small manger could fit on your dining room or kitchen table to serve as a reminder of the One who is coming. Can you light candles every night you read this Advent devotional?

You may also take a special look at any mangers that are part of the crèche or nativity sets that you have in your home. What do you notice? What animals come to eat at the manger of the nativity scene?

Pray

God of angels and sheep, God of the poor and meek
God of bright shining stars and God of babies asleep.
Quiet us to hear where new life is struggling to be born.
Slow our rush so we may notice the humble
and poor around us.
Fill our hearts with anticipation and our voices with song.

✳ SECOND WEEK ✳

From the Second Manger to Contemporary Expression

Introduction

In the first week, we met Saint Francis at the midnight outdoor celebration and re-enactment of the birth of Jesus. This week, we cross the centuries to see how the Bethlehem story has been relived and reimagined in the customs and traditions of our Advent and Christmas actions and rituals.

You may want to pray this prayer for the beginning of the week. Let it inspire your words and prayers.

Holy One, come. Lift our eyes from lists to see the wonders of the heavens and the smiles on each other's face. Fill our hearts with carols of joy, songs of gladness. Make conflicts cease, fill each table with sufficient food, and shelter us from the cold and dark. Holy One, come with forgiveness and healing. And make us just wild enough to sing in the midst of troubles, hope in the midst of doubts, and light candles in the midst of every darkness. Amen.

Second Sunday of Advent

Gather around your Advent wreath and share these reflections and prayers.

If you did not make an Advent wreath last week and would like to do so, check the instructions from last Sunday and make an Advent wreath for you, your family, or friends to use each evening (or other designated time) for the ritual of prayer and candle lighting.

Please change the personal pronouns as needed to make the prayers speak to you.

Centering Time

Take a few deep breaths. Breathe in hope with each inhale. Breathe out any fears with each exhale. Breathe in hope, let go of fear.

Pray

Cause us to breathe deep, Loving God, just for this moment, a letting go of worry and anxiety about all that's left to do. Center us in your amazing grace so that we may hear the flutter of angel wings, know the gift of your peace, receive the gift of our healing, and live in the grace of your forgiveness.

May each breath open us to the simple and beautiful ways you are with us. Raise us in your hope, promise to be with us, and open us to the Child who comes to love us. Amen.

Reading

Choose from Malachi 3:1-4; Luke 1:68-79; Philippians 1:3-11; or Luke 3:1-5.

These are lessons often used on the second Sunday of Advent. They may have been used in a worship service that you attended today. You may wish to explore the readings using different translations and having different readers.

Candle Lighting

Light two candles on the Advent wreath.

Prayer: *One candle can chase away the darkness. Two candles can light two rooms or be held by two persons. May the growing brightness spread to a wider community in need of more light and hope. May this light also touch more spaces within the rooms of my inner darkness. Loving God, may these two candles symbolize a growing awareness of your love and work in our world and my commitment to sharing the light that entered at the manger in Bethlehem.*

Prayers

Lift up any joys or concerns in a time of prayer.

One pattern of sharing encourages the person praying to say, "This is my prayer" after mentioning an intention for a person or situation. Others then may respond, "This is our prayer."

I encourage you to use this pattern or discover a pattern that works for you.

A Look Ahead

Before concluding your prayers around the Advent wreath, briefly review your coming week. Notice any events, meetings, or activities that you may want to hold in prayer as part of your daily reading and reflection.

Day One

Candles and Light

On that night in Greccio, Italy, where Francis gathered the towns-folk for the reenactment of the Bethlehem moment, the men, women, and children prepared candles and torches to light up the night. I imagine a scene with people walking carefully over well-known but now shadowy paths toward the cave, with flaming torches and high anticipation. Hopefully, it was a clear night with stars shining above as the additional glow of the villagers' torches lit up the clearing for the holy man of God, standing before the manger, and telling of the birth of the poor King who would bring light, joy, and peace to the world. In that dark corner of the world, those in attendance experienced a festive night of light.

Little is known about the origins of candles, but many believe that candles have been around for over five thousand years. The Romans are generally credited with the first wick candles. They dipped rolled papyrus repeatedly into melted beeswax or tallow. In India, they used a residue from boiling the fruit of the cinnamon tree. The Egyptians, Chinese, and Japanese also had wick candles from before the birth of Christ. More interesting information can be found at the National Candle Association.

The Bible has numerous references to lampstands or candle-sticks, many relating to temple worship, while broader images of light and dark permeate scripture. Psalm 119:105 reminds us that God's word is like a candle. "Your word is a lamp to my feet and a light to my path." Psalm 18:28 testifies, "It is you who lights my lamp; the LORD, my God, lights up my darkness." Jesus tells us not to hide our candle, our light, under a bushel but to let our light shine. (See Matthew 5:15.) Jewish Hanukkah, the Festival of Lights, dates back to 165 BCE.

The Advent tradition we are using in this study is common, though many traditions also add a center candle representing Christ. The wreath—circular to represent the eternity of God—holds four candles, usually purple or blue. Purple represents the penitential and prayerful traditions associated with preparing for the Christ's coming. Fasting, in particular, was suggested as a way to prepare for the coming of Christ. Blue candles are now as common as purple, partly to distinguish Advent from the season of Lent and also to suggest a time of great anticipation and waiting. Whether purple or blue are used, the third candle is usually pink or rose to mark a halfway point in the journey and to remind us of the joy that is coming.

Advent candles seem to have their origin in Germany and Scandinavia, often from Lutheran traditions. Advent candles brought light to a dark time of the year and also provided a way to count the Sundays to Christmas. One nineteenth century description at a German mission school had four large white candles interspersed with six smaller red candles to mark all the days leading to Christmas. By the early 1900s, Advent wreaths and candles were used in churches in the United States.

The four candles often have themes or characters associated with them: hope, peace, joy (the third Sunday of Advent and the rose candle in most sets), and love are the most common. The candles represent Isaiah, John the Baptist, Mary, and Joseph in another theme. Churches often vary the themes and sing songs that change the order or created new themes since the candles and the Sundays provide a vehicle to tell the story of God's love for creation. You may wish to choose a word or image for each candle. Saint Francis was fond of befriending all of creation, claiming Brother Sun and Sister Moon as his kin. Maybe your candles can become companions and kin on your journey.

Besides loving to look at dancing candle flames and enjoying the way flickering candles do indeed light up a darkened room, I have welcomed the way the home candle wreath mirrors often larger candle wreaths in church. It is a way to link church and home, faith community and family unit in all its variety.

Ponder

Who lights a candle for you in your darkness? Who shines light onto your path? Give thanks for the persons in your life who provide light for you to find your way.

Where in the world is there a need for candles of hope? Remember those places in prayer.

Who is a spark for you, someone who starts you thinking or dreaming or planning?

What scripture passage is a light for your path?

Light two candles if you have not previously done so.

Pray

Holy One, come be light for our darkness. Come shine in our homes and in our hearts. Come be a candle of hope for those in the darkness of poverty, for those huddled in fear of wars swirling around them, for those wondering about their next meal. Come, be a guide for our path and a beacon for our way. Amen.

Day Two

Music and Longing

At the first manger, Luke records that shepherds were the first to hear the news of the birth of a Savior. "And suddenly there was with the angel a multitude of the heavenly host, praising God and saying, 'Glory to God in the highest heaven, and on earth peace among those whom he favors!'" (Luke 2:13-14).

At the second manger, there was also singing. Thomas wrote that the brothers of Francis were singing praises as the people arrived, and the whole evening was filled with jubilation. We have learned that Francis, in his younger and partying days, was not only fun to be with but also a good singer. On that torchlit evening, he sang the holy gospel of the birth. "Here is his voice: a powerful voice, a pleasant voice, a clear voice, a musical voice, inviting all to the highest of gifts."[1]

It is hard to imagine Christmas without music. Many people have grown up with favorite Christmas carols that they sing during the season. While I was serving churches, people were eager to sing Christmas carols and hymns, even as many others lamented the generic Christmas music that played in stores many weeks before Christmas. The challenge for pastors was to honor the season of Advent, with its themes of preparation, while knowing many members of the congregation wanted to sing "Silent Night" and "O Little Town of Bethlehem" way before December 25.

Thankfully, we are blessed with wonderful Advent songs that easily enter into our hearts and souls, deepening our spiritual journey to Christmas. These Advent hymns articulate our deep longing for the coming birth and for our world to be different with the coming again of Christ.

"Come, Thou Long-Expected Jesus" by Charles Wesley, though not a new hymn, is one of the Advent hymns that comes readily to mind as we turn to music for the season before Christmas. Wesley names our longing for freedom, especially to be free from our fears and our sins. Scripture records many times when people in the time of Jesus hear the words "do not be afraid." An angel tells Mary to not be afraid to bear the Christ child. (See Luke 1:30.) Joseph hears in a dream not to be afraid to take Mary as his wife. (See Matthew 1:20.) The angels tell the shepherds not to be afraid, for the angels were bringing good news of great joy for all people. (See Luke 2:10.) Over one hundred other times in both the Hebrew scriptures and the New Testament, we find various expressions of the admonition to "not be afraid."

What other things do we long for? Perhaps we long for freedom from our prejudices, snap judgments, and our quick tempers that tend to get us in trouble. We long for a release from anxiety and worry so that we can rest—truly rest—in the embrace of our loving God. We long for healing of wounds and hurts, both physical and emotional, that keep us from living each day with hope and joy. We long for the dawning of forgiveness and for peace to guide our steps. We long for the return of kindness as a way of human interaction and for a generous respect of differences and diversity.

Beyond the interpersonal, we long for a new reign of peace and civility where disagreements and challenges become opportunities for new partnerships and for considering the welfare of those without power or voice. We long for wars to cease, weapons to be laid down, and every land mine to be safely plucked up and destroyed before it harms another child at play. We long for all to be fed, that in God's world of abundance, we learn to share. We long for creation to be cherished, rivers and streams to be clear, the air to be breathable.

So many longings. Come, thou long expected Jesus, touch our longings with the hope of a new day.

Ponder

What would your list of longings look like? Personal, interpersonal, professional, societal?

Who is making a difference in the world and creating new spaces of respect or learning or healing or recovery or reconciliation? Consider sending a letter to someone who is making a difference in the world and thank the person for the work he or she is doing.

Light two candles. Sing or read the words of the Advent hymn, "Come, Thou Long Expected Jesus."

Pray

Come to us, Child of God. Come as peace to our troubled world; come as comfort to all who grieve; come as childlike joy excited about the wonder of the season. Come as hope for a better day for those times we've lost our way. Come to us, Child in a manger, and raise in us our hopes and our songs. Amen.

Day Three

Music and Anticipation

While our longing often points to something distant that lingers in the future, anticipation seems closer at hand, something that is going to happen and happen soon.

Francis asked his good friend John to prepare for the reenactment of the story of Jesus' birth. Though no amount of wishing or begging by a young child can make December 25 arrive any faster, there are things one can do to prepare for the celebration.

Between Thanksgiving and the first Sunday of Advent, it is time at our house to bring out the decorations for Christmas. These decorations include manger or crèche sets (I use both words interchangeably to describe a nativity scene representing the birth of Christ, crèche being a French word for a manger or nativity scene), the Advent wreath, Christmas dishes, and our favorite Christmas mugs. As we make the shift from ordinary time and our usual décor, I get out the Christmas music, CDs, and a few cherished cassette tapes. The music sets the environment for the change of seasons, ranging from monks chanting to carols from the Celtic tradition. When he was a child, our son liked a CD of music box carols. Now that he's grown, he prefers Stevie Wonder's Christmas album. Our daughter has shifted from Amy Grant's music to that of the Indigo Girls. I am glad to have a Christmas CD from Josh Groban. Whatever your favorite style of Christmas music, there is most likely a way to download or purchase it from the internet, or get out the old CDs.

The Advent hymn, "O Come, O Come, Emmanuel" marries the longing for wisdom that orders "all things far and nigh," the longing for the Dayspring that cheers us, disperses the "gloomy clouds of night," and puts death's dark shadows to flight with the assurance that the longing will be fulfilled. The majestic refrain announces the good news, "Rejoice! Rejoice! Emmanuel shall come to thee, O Israel." What we prepare for, what we anticipate and long and pray for, "shall come." It shall come.

Ponder

What Christmas music or song names your longing or lifts your spirits? Can you plan time to listen to some of your favorite Christmas music? Is there a concert or musical in the holiday season that you want to add to your calendar?

How do you put your house in order so that you may receive the coming Christ child with a new openness and receptivity?

What would it take to develop a practice so that every time you hear holiday music in stores, it serves as a call to prayer and becomes an opportunity for preparation?

Light two candles and sing an Advent song.

Pray

O come, O come, Emmanuel and fill our hearts with carols of joy and songs of gladness. Come bring healing to bodies and souls hurt by abuse, by addictions, or by bitter words. Shower us with forgiveness and blessings, hope, and laughter. Let your love clothe us as frost on the morning grass. Make us bold and crazy enough to sing our hope with loud voices and whole hearts in the face of despair or death's dark shadows or gloomy nights of fear. O come, O come, Emmanuel. Amen.

Day Four

Trees

Francis loved God's creation. His most famous prayer begins by addressing Brother Sun and Sister Moon and adds many other sisters and brothers of creation. Francis walked everywhere in central Italy and found prayer places in the hills, the caves, and the forests of Umbria. It made sense to Francis to celebrate the Holy Baby's birth outdoors. Again, according to Thomas of Celano, "The people arrive, ecstatic at this new mystery of new joy. The forest amplifies the cries and the boulders echo back the joyful crowd."[2]

The evergreen tree has long been a symbol of life in the midst of the darkness of winter in northern climes. In pagan traditions, evergreens served as a reminder that the sun god and warmth would return again. The Celts and Romans decorated their homes and temples with evergreen boughs for the Winter Solstice. Ancient inhabitants of northern Europe cut fir and pine trees and planted them in boxes inside their homes in wintertime.

Germany is credited with starting the Christmas tree tradition in the sixteenth century when devout Christians brought decorated trees into their homes. It is believed Martin Luther was the first to place a candle on the tree as he sought to capture the brilliance of starlight shining through the winter evergreens he glimpsed on evening walks.

Queen Victoria of England popularized placing gifts under and even on the tree as she, Prince Albert, and her children were pictured in a journal standing around a fir tree. As the Queen does, so did many others. In the United States, trees were not as popular until the nineteenth century when President Pierce placed a tree in the White House and Clement Moore wrote *Twas the Night before Christmas*. Such images in popular culture have clearly had an impact as over thirty-five million evergreens make their appearance in our homes, churches, and public spaces each year—and that does not count the ten million artificial trees purchased each year in the United States.

Nearly every year, our family has ventured out in December to cut down a Christmas tree. We started this tradition when a parishioner invited us to her fifteen-acre farm to cut one. Since that year in Michigan, we have cut down trees in Southern California when there was no snow in sight, and Massachusetts, where there was plenty of snow and it was freezing cold. We have ornaments from family and friends, and each one tells a story that leads us to remember people and places as we decorate. We do not use candles like Luther did, but the colored lights we use twinkle like stars, especially late at night with the regular lights turned off. The sights and the smells are part of our Advent preparation.

Though the pagan sun god is no longer part of Christian celebrations at Christmas, the evergreen as a symbol of everlasting life remains present. While most landscapes in northern habitats are brown, the evergreen—with its fragrance and bright green color— exists as a cheery and constant sign of hope for the greening of new life. I suspect the Christmas tree will remain an ever-present tradition in many homes and places of worship.

Ponder

Tell another person the stories of Christmas trees from your family history. Do you have particular memories? (One year, the fully-decorated tree fell on me as I was lifting up the branches to add water to the Christmas tree stand!)

What is your earliest memory of a Christmas tree in your family?

If you wrote a prayer about creation, what would you call a favorite tree? Brother, Sister, Grandfather, Grandmother? Some other term of affection? Write your prayer and share it with another person.

The Giving Tree by Shel Silverstein and *The Tale of Three Trees: A Traditional Folktale* by Angela Elwell Hunt are a couple of books you may want to read. Light two Advent candles.

Pray

God of creation, lover of trees with their branches reaching to the heavens and their roots embracing the earth, thank you for all kinds of trees. Especially, thank you for evergreen trees that show they are alive in the depths of winter, whose green brings color to our brown and barren earth. Thank you for Christmas trees with sparkling lights, shiny balls, and tinsel, an amazing pillar of light and joy and wonder. Thank you for wonder and beauty and the abiding hope that·you will lift our spirits up to the realm of singing angels. Amen.

Day Five

Crèche Sets

Luke's Gospel records in two places in chapter two that the Child was wrapped in cloth and lying in a manger. Francis is so taken by the image of Jesus in a manger that he wished to see with his own eyes the manger, the hay, the ox, the ass, and the discomfort of the Holy Child.

Francis's interest in the nativity is not so surprising when one reads about his life. It is easy to see how Francis, with his whole heart and intention, sought to follow not only the teachings of Jesus but also to retrace the footsteps and humility of the Savior. He meditated on the words of Christ, spending long hours in prayer. He sought to live a life of simplicity so that no attachments would get in his way of joyfully serving the poor, the least, and the lost. His initial encounter and embrace of the leper forever shaped his compassion.

Francis, a joyful servant of God, attracted a following. The jubilant Christmas Eve service in Greccio forever changed the way many of us celebrate Christmas. It is common in the weeks leading to Christmas to find nativity sets with ceramic figures, children in Christmas pageants centered around a manger, or live nativity displays in front of churches.

In Francis's day, the Roman Catholic mass was said in Latin, so many churchgoers depended on visuals and storytelling to learn about characters from the Bible. Mystery or miracle plays were common, popular forms of education and entertainment performed in churches and town squares in the local language of the people. Francis's visual display of the manger not only told the story but also invited people to identify with and emotionally connect with the Babe of Bethlehem born in a manger. God made flesh in a child would need the people to care and love for the Holy One in their midst.

Not long after the night in Greccio, other churches staged reenactments of the Nativity story. This popular type of theater spread across Italy and beyond. Later, statues and figurines added to and sometimes even replaced the live reenactments. It was not always easy to find cooperative sheep, oxen, or camels. The large outdoor dramas moved inside churches and often took on the flavor of the local community with handcrafted figures in flowing robes in the style of the village. In the mid 1500s, nativity sets moved inside homes and sometimes remained on display for the whole year.

Our family collection of crèche sets comes from many of the countries we have visited as well as distinctive sets that appealed to one member of the family, usually me. I enjoy a set from Mexico given to us by a church member. The set has a female angel dressed in a Mexican robe. A set from Kenya, dark wood for faces and limbs with light-colored wood for the robes and clothes, always receives a special display spot. The El Salvador crèche glows with vivid colors, lots of bright reds and yellows. The crèche we purchased in Portugal is painted on a pottery roof shingle. The German nativity is a wooden merry-go-round with four candles providing updraft that propels the blades to spin the Holy Family round and round.

One from the Czech Republic came to us in our son's backpack after a year of traveling—I feel the long journey was part of the gift.

As we set up each one, we remember the country, visit, or person who gave the nativity and how the birth of Jesus touches many countries and people.

Ponder

If you have a nativity set or sets, tell the story of how they came to be with you. Do you have a special place for them in your home? Give thanks for the memories that they stir.

Explore or inquire if there are any living nativities in your area and if so, schedule a time to visit on one of the days or evenings they are outside. Dress warmly if you are in a cold climate.

Would you wish to make or purchase a nativity set for your home? Some handcraft and trade organizations offer nativity sets from many different countries. Ten Thousand Villages is one organization that has shops and a catalogue of gifts including manger sets.

Light two candles if you have not previously done so.

Pray

Coming God, make our hearts open and our homes ready to receive the miracle of your birth. Help us to clear away the unnecessary, put aside the unimportant, and lay down the unrealistic so we can hear the angel songs and see the miracles in the common and ordinary. Cut our lists in half, and help us to say the appropriate "no" to the one more task. Open us to the moments of silence and the whispers of grace. Amen.

Weekend Activity

This weekend is a good time to hang some outdoor Christmas lights at your home. Outside decorating can be as simple as hanging a strand of lights around your door or maybe a strand inside around a window. Many people also put electric candles in the windows, a sign that your house is ready to receive the Christ child. Many Christmas lights are now energy-efficient with LED bulbs.

If you have not already added a Christmas tree to your preparations, this could be a good weekend to go to a Christmas tree farm or a Christmas tree lot. Even in warm climates, there are places to cut down a tree or to visit a church or non-profit that sells Christmas trees to raise funds, often for mission projects. As you decorate the tree, play some Christmas music and tell stories about the decorations that you put on your tree. Some families have a tradition of decorating the tree on Christmas Eve, but I can never wait that long. Also, I love the smell of evergreen in the house. (Many communities also have days to recycle trees after the holidays. It is always a good practice to recycle.)

Setting up your crèche sets can be a meditative practice, a way of prayer for opening to the coming of God to our lives and our world. If you have your nativities already set up, this could be a week to move the magi closer to the manger. It is a way to mark the days getting closer to the birth.

You might also see if there is a living nativity in your area and visit it this weekend. Some cities or churches also have collections of nativity sets. I remember visiting a church in Montreal over a Thanksgiving trip and discovering a large collection of nativities from around the world. The Upper Room Chapel and Museum has a wonderful collection of nativities from many countries. Another time, I visited the Tucson Museum of Art's historic Casa Cordova that displays a single nativity, El Nacimiento (the birth), from November to March. El Nacimiento has over 800 pieces depicting not only the Christmas story but other biblical stories as well.

Pray

Generous God, you are unfolding a new a new blessing for us and for the world. Help us pay attention to
   the movements of Grace,
   the tremors of Love,
   the ripples of Hope,
   the whispers of Peace,
   today and every day. Amen.

The Living Nativity in Global and Personal Context

Introduction

Christianity, the world's largest religion with over 2.2 billion adherents, celebrates the birth of Jesus with local flavor around the world. Some of the practices, like Christmas trees and nativity sets with European roots, have found a permanent home in American culture. As the United States grows more diverse, Christmas traditions from other countries are finding a home in our current celebrations.

As appreciation for other traditions increases, many Christians are also becoming more concerned about the commercialization of the holiday. There is a longing for a quieter, simpler, and more prayerful way to prepare for the birth of the Christ child. Saint Francis's love for the Child of Bethlehem led him to deep prayer and a desire to simply follow the humble Jesus. He became like his prayer and once wrote, "Where there is peace and contemplation, there is neither care (anxiety in another transla-tion) nor restlessness."[1]

This week we look at the interweaving of these themes as we experience a Christmas more diverse and more spiritual, more col-orful and more reflective, more expressive and more compassionate.

You may want to pray this prayer for the beginning of the week. Let it inspire your words and prayers.

God of hope and joy, go with us this week and all of our days and help us know and believe that the day is coming when all shall sing, and all shall hear a Baby's cry. A day is coming when those grieving shall be comforted, when the weak will become strong, and when the angels will sing. A day is coming when shepherds will run, gifts will be given, and carols will be sung. Remind us that it won't be long until we will know this coming joy. For one day, for all days. Amen.

Third Sunday of Advent

Gather around your Advent wreath and share reflections and prayers.

Please change the personal pronouns as needed to make the prayers speak to you.

Centering Time

Take a few deep breaths. Breathe in joy with each inhale. Breathe out sorrow with each exhale. Breathe in joy, let go of sadness.

Pray

Cause us to breathe deep, Loving God, just for this moment, a letting go of worry and anxiety about all that's left to do. Center us in your amazing grace so that we may hear the flutter of angel wings, know the gift of your peace, receive the gift of our healing, and live in the grace of your forgiveness.

May each breath open us to the simple and beautiful ways you are with us. Raise us in your joy and promise to be with us and open us to the Child who comes to love us. Amen.

Reading

Choose from Zephaniah 3:14-20; Isaiah 12:2-6; Philippians 4:4-7; or Luke 3:7-18.

These are lessons often used on the third Sunday of Advent. They may have been used in a worship service that you attended today. You may wish to explore the readings using different translations and having different readers. Notice the themes of joy that permeate the lessons. Sing for joy and do not be afraid—a wonderful word for lighting the joy candle this week.

Candle Lighting

Light three candles on the Advent wreath. If you are using a pink or rose-colored candle in your set, this is the Sunday and week to light this candle of joy. The third week is intended to provide a break in the more somber, penitential observance of Advent.

Prayer: *Amazing God, let some joy loose this week. Let it rise to the surface and shake us out of preoccupation with lists and tasks. Forgive us for a heavy-hearted approach to your season of joy and light. Help us not to let long lists and calendar events overwhelm the wonder of your birth. Smiling God, let some joy loose in us, and let it rub off on others.*

Prayers

Lift up any joys or concerns in a time of prayer.

One pattern of sharing encourages the person praying to say, "This is my prayer" after mentioning an intention for a person or situation. Others then may respond, "This is our prayer."

You are encouraged to use this pattern or discover a pattern that works for you.

A Look Ahead

Before concluding your prayers around the Advent wreath, briefly look at your coming week. Notice any events, meetings, or activities that you may want to hold in prayer as part of your daily reading and reflection.

Day One

Las Posadas

I served a bilingual English-Spanish church in southeast Los Angeles for a number of years. Thankfully, I shared the ministry with a humble and compassionate bilingual pastor who had grown up in Mexico and who was patient with my study of Spanish. He was more than willing to introduce a young minister from Michigan to the gifts and spirituality of Latin people. I am richer because of those years with Rev. David Tinoco, and my ministry became more sensitive to and appreciative of people from other countries.

One Christmas, David and the Spanish-speaking members of the congregation took me on Las Posadas, a visit to The Inns. This nine-day tradition began in the villages of Mexico where children, dressed as angels, Mary, or Joseph, lead a procession that walks to neighbors' homes in a search for safe shelter for the Holy Family to have their child. Each night ends at a home where there is food, songs, and scripture. The nine days represent the nine months that Mary was pregnant.

In the sprawling city of Los Angeles, the nine nights were reduced to fit contemporary schedules and reality. This particular Sunday night, we traveled by cars. While members of each home led us in a song, scripture, and prayer, it was at the last home where the time of worship turned into a fabulous feast and celebration. I learned about traditional foods—empanadas, tamales, and beans—and I learned that the children looked forward to hitting a piñata, a hollow papier-mâché shape filled with candies. Thirty-five years ago, these traditions were all new to me; yet now the foods are part of our cuisine and many children's parties have birthday piñatas.

Las Posadas is a direct lineage from what Saint Francis sought to do in Greccio. Each experience takes the story of Jesus' birth and translates it into a participatory experience, a dramatization of scripture. The second manger at Greccio and the Las Posadas in Mexico and Los Angeles make the Bethlehem story real. The story of the Incarnation takes root amongst the ordinary folk.

The joyous tradition highlights the precarious situation of a poor Holy Land family looking for safe shelter in a country ruled by an imperial power. Many people on the margins—immigrants, and the poor—know what it's like to search for shelter and for a place to call home. The prophet Zephaniah says God wants to bring the exiles home and restore them as a people who know blessing. (See Zephaniah 3:20.) The joy of this third week of Advent is found in the vision of coming home, finding safe shelter, and rejoicing in community.

While I was on a sabbatical study leave, I lived in a Quaker community outside of Philadelphia. One of the community members organized a contemporary Las Posadas. Two members of the community dressed as Mary and Joseph, and we walked to various buildings on the campus, knocked at doors, and looked for shelter. We ended up being welcomed in the garbage area by two poor folk (community members playing their parts) who offered their card-board box and a few crackers to Mary and Joseph as the rest of us watched in uncomfortable, yet prayerful, silence.

Saint Francis would have understood the poverty and humilia-tion of having to give birth in a stable. He embraced poverty as a follower of Christ and crossed the barrier to the outcasts when he embraced a leper. It was a conversion moment for Francis, and it happens for us every time we remember our kinship with all cre-ation. We embrace Christ when we care for the least, the lost, and the forgotten.

Ponder

Reflect on the homes in which you have lived and how they have or have not been places of safety for you.

What traditions from around the world are part of your Christ-mas celebrations? Are there foods or customs that now feel familiar to you when once they were new and strange?

Where will you experience joy this Advent, and will this joy involve community and food?

Is there a refugee, immigrant, or poor family that you can befriend this season? How might you learn their story?

How can you make your celebration of Christmas simpler and become more aware of the poor in the world?

Pray

God of the journey, send your angels near, for we are in need of your guidance. We stumble in the dark, choose the wrong paths, and follow after the wrong gods. Success lures us. Quick schemes tempt us. Strang-ers frighten us. Oh, whisper words that help us know the way to go.

God of the last house, send your angels near, for we are in need of your joy that is shared with family and community, joy that includes the poor and the foreigner, the young and the old.

God of whispers and dreams, send your angels near and fill us with courage to continue to love others, do justice, and walk humbly on this good earth. Amen.

Day Two

Calendars, Chains, and Cards

Calendars, paper chains, and cards are all ways to keep the preparation and anticipation of Christmas present each day. Celano notes that Saint Francis sought to think only about the things of the Lord. Indeed, Francis was consumed with knowing scripture and encouraging those who followed him to do the same. I believe he would have marveled at the ways we keep Bible verses in front of us in calendars, paper chains, and cards. Most of us need these kinds of hints, objects, habits, and traditions to keep the coming of the Christ child present for us and for others.

We have Europe to thank for Advent paper traditions that are now so common to our preparations for Christmas. Advent calendars are a popular way to count down to Christmas, but one of the first counting strategies reported by early nineteenth century German Protestants used chalk to mark the twenty-four days and erased a chalk line every day until Christmas.

The first paper calendars printed were made in the mid-nineteenth century, most likely in Germany. Early calendars had Bible verses or biblical pictures behind each paper window. Winter images such as snowflakes and toys were also common.

Handmade calendars were no doubt created much earlier than the printed ones.

In our home, we have a large felt calendar with twenty-four sewn pockets. Each pocket is decorated with a Christmas or Christian symbol, from crosses to mangers to stars to candles. Each pocket holds a three-by-five-inch note card that has a suggested activity for the day or a Bible verse or a song to sing. Though our children are grown, we still hang the calendar. However, I confess we no longer draw out a card each day and follow the suggestion.

Churches that I have been part of also have provided Advent calendars for the church family, though gluing little windows to cover the activity or verse for the day can be labor intensive. Churches also have used such calendars as a prayer practice with a member or family or world situation named as the focus for prayer. Another time, a church made an Advent chain with twenty-five strips of purple, blue, and pink paper. Each strip contained a Bible verse or activity. Children enjoyed the task of gluing and linking the strips together, and each family or child had an Advent chain to take home to count down the days to Christmas. Most purchased Advent calendars, even the ones with chocolate behind each window, do not follow the four weeks of Advent. Instead, they begin on December 1. If you try to use them with the four Sundays of Advent, you may be short a couple of days.

Advent calendars, wreaths, and chains are tools to help us mark time. Each of us has the same amount of time—twenty-four hours in a day—but time can get away from us, overwhelm us, and be wasted by us. Managing time seems important, but doing so often feels too structured and does not yield well to interruptions or changes. Finding ways to mark our days, to keep awake to the beauty and wonder around us, and to be open to surprise and nuance is a challenge and an opportunity for all of us. The four weeks of Advent and the ways of marking each day can prepare our hearts for the miracle of the Babe of Bethlehem.

Christmas cards that arrive help nurture a heart that is open to surprise and blessing. Awaiting the mail and anticipating a card or package was a wonderful feeling as a child. Especially as the children's grandparents lived some distance away, the box of cookies and the cards with money were highlights of the season.

The first Christmas cards were probably mass-produced in England in the 1830s. They were small cards featuring festive scenes and prewritten greetings. Again, handwritten notes and cards preceded the production of the greeting card as we know it. With the advent of email and other electronic and video communication, we are seeing fewer cards arrive. My handwritten epistles with news of our family from years past have been replaced with my words now typed, edited, and combined with photos of the family and emailed to people near and far. They are beautiful, thoughtful, and newsy, but a part of me misses the evenings with Christmas music when I added notes to the cards or letters that I stuffed into envelopes and stamped. Thankfully, others have resurrected card making as a creative endeavor and children still enjoy creating art that graces many family cards.

Ponder

What ways do you mark the journey to Christmas now and what ways do you recall from an earlier time?

How do you mark time? What tools do you use to keep a balance of attention to tasks while remaining open to surprise?

Mark Nepo writes in his book, *The One Life We're Given*, about the inevitable struggle between what we intend and what life provides. He suggests this is the challenge as we move through each day. It is an art to intentionally mark time and enjoy the moment. How is your art?

Imagine that Saint Francis sends you a Christmas card. What blessings of creation and which verses of scripture would he send to you?

Pray

Holy One, Coming One,
    teach us to mark our days with joy and anticipation,
    with open hearts and expectant souls.

Remind us that
    beyond the darkness there is a star,
    beyond the noise there is an angel song,
    beyond the rush there is a wondrous silence.

Holy One, Coming One, attune our lives and our ears and our eyes to your presence in every moment, your comfort in every sigh, your peace in every minute. Amen.

Day Three

Labyrinths and Spirals

In the thirteenth century, walking was the usual mode of travel, and it offered time for reflection and conversation. In a preserved letter from Saint Francis to Brother Leo, Francis sums up their conversation on the road from Assisi to LaVerna, which is about one hundred and thirty miles. "In whatever way you think you will best please our Lord God and follow in his footsteps and in poverty, take that way with the Lord God's blessing and my obedience."[2]

Today, we have designated labyrinths as places for reflection and prayer. At the same time, the growing interest in pilgrimages—especially walking the Camino de Santiago in Spain—testifies to our desire to walk and pray, to walk and converse without time pressures.

Generally, a labyrinth is a circuitous path that leads to a center. Its design is found in many ancient civilizations, on walls, coins, or in fields. Labyrinths found new interest in the work of Episcopalian priest Lauren Artress, who discovered a labyrinth in the floor of the Chartres Cathedral in France. In medieval times, when it was too long and dangerous to travel to the Holy Land, pilgrims could visit one of the great cathedrals and walk the labyrinth as their prayer.

Today, many churches, hospitals, schools, and spiritual centers have labyrinths on their property. Their presence encourages people to make a meditative, prayerful walk to the center. Walking helps focus one's mind and provides an openness to standing or sitting in the center of the labyrinth. Often people will walk with an intention or question on their heart on their way to the center. The center space provides a time and place to rest, pray, and think, while walking out is an opportunity to release, let go, or make a resolve.

Advent provides a holy tradition of preparation, and the labyrinth invites people to slow down, place one foot in front of the other, and walk slowly toward the center. An Advent labyrinth walk helps one let go of long lists and a constant flurry of activity. (A resource to help you find a labyrinth near you is included at the end of this chapter in the Weekend Activity.)

While serving a church in Southern California, we scheduled an early evening labyrinth walk. We placed candles at the places of turning and around the edges. We invited a guitarist to play Christmas music while the folks walked prayerfully toward the center.

The growing darkness, the candles, and the music created an environment of quiet contemplation.

Before the creation of the outdoor labyrinth at the church, we offered an evening of prayer by walking a spiral that we laid down inside the church. I got the idea from a church in Washington that used evergreen branches to form a spiral path leading to an open space in the center. We placed candles in cored apples and invited participants to place their apple along the path and to offer prayer. We left the spiral up for a week between Sundays and invited people to come anytime to walk and pray. The apples let people know that prayers had been offered.

It is good to know that prayers have been offered as we walk the paths of life.

The prophet Isaiah encourages us to trust and not be afraid, for God is our strength and salvation. Whether we walk a labyrinth, a spiral, or just take a long prayerful walk in a neighborhood or along a stream or in a forest, a walk can be a fruitful time of reflection on the Holy Child who comes to us where we are.

Ponder

Remember a walk that brought stillness to the mind, clarity to a concern, and openness to the heart. Give thanks.

Schedule a time to walk a labyrinth. Google "labyrinth locator" to find a labyrinth near you.

Light three candles on your Advent wreath, including the pink candle.

Pray

God of the journey, walk with us as we dash through the ordinary and weave through the busyness. Help us overcome roadblocks and detours as we make our way home to you. Help us leave the past in the past

*as we move from darkness and exile into light and community. Let this
Advent be our path to you, a way to come home to you and to our true
self. Amen.*

Day Four ·

Peace Letters

For most of the years of our marriage, my wife and I hosted an
Advent gathering. It served to connect our church family with col-
leagues and friends beyond the church in an afternoon and evening of food and conversation. It also carried out our belief that the
church house (a parsonage or manse in some traditions) we lived
in was a blessing for us and was open to the congregation—usually
at designated times and gatherings. Though it can be abused, the
Spanish expression "mi casa es su casa," translated "my house is
your house," has literally been true for most of our married life.

Though Christmas often focuses on the family and gifts, there
dwells a constant theme that the Child of Bethlehem is for the
whole world. The angels announce that the good news of great joy
is, "for all people" and the heavenly choir sings, "Glory to God in
the highest heaven and on earth peace, good will among people"
(Luke 2:10, 14). There is a global and life-changing, world-chang-
ing context to this Birth in Bethlehem.

While many believe that the story of the Incarnation is about
God coming to save fallen humankind, other early writers, like
Irenaeus of Lyons, saw the Incarnation more as the completion
of God's intention for creation rather than a payback for the
sin of Adam and Eve. Indeed, the followers of Francis believed
that the "Incarnation occurs because of a positive—love—not a

negative—sin."[3] In the Incarnation, the humble God in the simple manger bends down to embrace and lift up creation to its intended glory. The mystery of the Incarnation for Francis was that God bends low in love to meet us where we are. Jesus—whose name was so dear to Francis on Christmas Eve that he could hardly use it, preferring instead "Babe from Bethlehem,"—was to be followed more than believed in. "The brothers who live with [Francis] know that daily, constantly, talk of Jesus was always on his lips. He was always with Jesus: Jesus in his heart, Jesus in his mouth, Jesus in his eyes, Jesus in his hands, he bore Jesus always in his whole body."[4] And God's love in Jesus was for everyone. Everyone.

At many of our Advent gatherings, we sought to embrace those who were working for peace across the globe by penning a letter and inviting our guests to add their names or comments. In our Advent file, I have treasured responses from some of the people we wrote, including Archbishop Dom Helder Camara of Brazil, Prime Minister Menachem Begin of Israel, and Anwar Sadat of Egypt in 1979, a time when they were working on peace in the Middle East. Also, Kurt Waldheim, the Secretary-General of the United Nations and Lech and Miroslawa Walesa, before Lech became the sixth President of Poland, are in the file. It is moving to examine the carefully folded letters and give thanks for their efforts to create a better world.

In 1219 during the Fifth Crusade, Francis and Brother Illuminato walked into the Muslim encampment and sought the Sultan, hoping for a way to bring peace. "May the Lord give you peace," said Francis. His standard greeting caught Sultan Malik al-Kamil by surprise and led to an extended stay in the tents of the enemy.[5] Despite threats to kill any Christians whom the Muslims caught, Francis and Illuminato walked out after nearly a year with a new appreciation of the prayer life of Muslims and the gift of an ivory horn used to call the Muslims to prayer five times a day. Francis sought a better world without crusades.

The story of Francis and our letter-writing past reminds me to rekindle the tradition and find new ways of building bridges to peace. Maybe letter writing is not just an Advent tradition, but also a forgotten blessing. To send notes of thanks and appreciation for the good that people do in the world, that is indeed a blessing. I confess that it is easier to send a quick email, but there is something extra special about taking the time to write. If God could and does bend low to be with us, I can share thanks and blessings with others.

Ponder

How does thinking of the Incarnation as a positive sign of love rather than the repayment of a debt change your sense of Christmas or the way you live out your faith?

Think about bending over a crib to lift a baby as an image of God's tender embrace of you and for all of creation. God is also the infant needing care. How do you hold the image of God Most High and God Most Humble?

Who is working for peace in the world and how could you send a word of encouragement? Some of these persons are not in the headlines but they should not be forgotten.

Pray

Loving God, Source of Joy and Peace, stir us to be people of peace. May our words and deeds reflect your desire for peace and justice. May our words be kind, our thoughts be hopeful, our actions be gentle, and our commitment be strong.

Grant us a joy that does not wear thin and a confidence that is beyond the results we see. Give us courage to speak truth, to stand for justice, and to see new paths to make peace.

Teach us to rekindle the light of hope for those who walk in darkness, and make us instruments of your peace. Amen.

Day Five

Blue Christmas—Longest Night

Anticipating Christmas joy sometimes masks the struggle and suffering that is present throughout life. "Francis's life was no picnic in the park. He understood and knew loss, pain, and suffering. He was in poor health most of his life once he was released from prison. He had only two desires when he thought of Christ's suffering: to know what Christ's sufferings were like and to know the love that gave Christ the courage to suffer."[6] Yet, Francis never let his suffering affect his celebration of Christmas. How do we balance joy and suffering as we approach Bethlehem?

The longest night of the year in the northern hemisphere is on or around December 21. A number of churches offer space or services for those for whom the festivities of the holiday season don't match with the experience of darkness and loss. For those reeling from the loss of loved ones or for those who have lost a job or relationship or received news of needed surgery or chemotherapy, or for those who are struggling with finances and family expectations, Christmas cheer seems a long way off. The present moments of sadness and disorientation make it hard to stomach the craziness and commercialization of the season.

After my father died in early December, our family went to a large downtown church for a Christmas Eve service. We occasionally attended this church, and I appreciated the large choir, added instruments, thoughtful liturgy, and good preaching. The opening processional song, "O Come, All Ye Faithful," with trumpet and timpani caused tears to flow and my words to hush. I was surprised by the emotion on this festive night, but my father loved to sing, and now he would not be in an earthly choir again. In the midst of loss, even when are doing well, we are often surprised by what triggers a memory that unleashes tears, mixed with both gratitude and loss.

Many churches choose the longest night to invite those with losses, plus family and friends, to come for a time of worship. Usually the services include readings from scripture and prayers, but a common element of most is the lighting of candles. Even in the darkest time of year, when sadness wraps its arms around us tight, we can gather to light candles of memory and candles of hope. Liturgy affirms that God is a God who knows our grief and invites us to walk through the valley of death, loss, and grief. We do not escape the valleys in our lifetime, but scripture points to moving through grief with the courage to mourn.

It may not only be personal loss that we grieve. We grieve with any person or group living through dark times in our cities, our countries, and our world. We may feel the pain of children traumatized by war, the loss of a species of animal, or the face of hunger in a land of plenty. Gathering together, praying, and lighting candles can bring healing and hope.

Ponder

Is there some loss that is current in your life right now? Is there some transition that would help you honor this loss with a prayer or a candle or an empty chair?

Who is going through a difficult time right now? How might you offer support? A phone call or text? A meal? An invite to a Longest Night service?

How do you wish to honor the longest night of the year?

Light three candles on your Advent wreath, including the pink candle.

Pray

Gracious God, we know and have known times of sadness and dark-ness, darkness within us and outside us. Though we do not cause light to shine, we can place ourselves in the path of your sunbeams, your star-light, the light of an Advent candle, and begin to experience the warmth of your presence, your love, and your healing. As we stand in your pres-ence, we can become light-bearers and hope-bringers to others. Grant us your touch and your light in these long nights. Amen.

Weekend Activity

The entries for this week carry many suggestions for Advent prepa-rations besides shopping.

Do you know of a Las Posadas walk you could join? Hispanic churches or sometimes sections of cities sponsor a version of a walk. While I lived near Los Angeles, we would take the children to the Mexican shopping district on Olvera Street, which spon-sored a Las Posadas. Children wore festive costumes, and Mariachi musicians led the way through the artisan shopping area.

This weekend might be a good time to locate a labyrinth and make a prayerful walk. Online, you can check Labyrinth Locator to see if there is a labyrinth near you that you could walk. Or you could gather pine branches and make a spiral walk in a church or a large courtyard.

Who in the midst of often discouraging news could use a note of encouragement for the work he or she is doing to make peace, build bridges, and bring reconciliation to our brokenness? If it is cold outside, a warm space to write a letter of warm affirmation would warm some leader's heart.

Who do you know who is going through some kind of loss? How might you respond? An offer of food—a home-cooked meal or from a restaurant—might get them out of a physical place of grief. A phone call or a card may comfort. Do they like humorous or sweet cards?

Pray

Holy One, Companion in our waiting
Help us to know that you do work to make the rough places
*   smooth;*
You do send angel choruses to lift our spirits;
You do place a brighter star on some blue-feeling night;
You do slip a prayer into our hearts that comforts and sustains.
Companion in our waiting, keep us alert to your surprises and
*   blessings. Amen.*

Heightened Anticipation

Introduction

Are we there yet? The familiar question from children in a car is easily rephrased to, "Is it Christmas yet?" Even with Advent calendars marking the twenty-five days and Advent wreaths marking the four weeks, the eagerness for Christmas is palpable.

Some of us feel anticipation for Christmas when we attend a children's Christmas pageant, complete with angel wings and shepherd bathrobes and memorized lines. For others, it is the midnight service with candlelight and singing "Silent Night." For many, it is gift giving and receiving and time with family and friends and good food and lots of cookies.

This week, we anticipate the arrival of the Baby of Bethlehem and some of the traditions that celebrate the Incarnation, the bending low of God to be with us through the humble and poor, the dark and cold, in the fields and in the streets, roads, lanes, avenues, or underpasses where we live.

You may want to pray this prayer for the beginning of the week. Let it inspire your words and prayers.

God of coming Joy, walk with us toward Bethlehem, looking for signs of your humble presence all around us, looking up for a new star to guide us, looking within for a hollowed-out space to receive your gift of love wrapped in a manger. It won't be long now until angel songs are heard and we find ourselves kneeling in wonder and awe. Keep us tender and open and ready to welcome joy and peace into our world and into our lives. Amen.

Depending on when you are reading this study, you may want to alter the readings to correspond with Christmas Eve and Christmas Day.

Fourth Sunday of Advent

Gather around your Advent wreath and share reflections and prayer.

Centering Time

Take a few deep breaths. Breathe in love with each inhale. Breathe out indifference with each exhale. Breathe in love, let go of hate.

Pray

Loving God, it won't be long now until a Child is born and angels sing and shepherds visit a King. It won't be long now until Silent Night is sung in candlelight. It won't be long now until children squirm in their beds with eager anticipation. It won't be long now until joy is unwrapped, feasts are shared, and a birth is remembered and celebrated.

It won't be long now, so ready the heart, quiet the rush, and open the soul to welcome the One who comes to break oppression, raise up the lowly, fill the hungry, and change the world. Thank you, Loving God, for journeying with us to Bethlehem. Amen.

Reading

Choose from Micah 5:2-5a; Luke 1:46b-55; Psalm 80:1-7; Hebrews 10:5-10; or Luke 1:39-45.

These are lessons often used on the fourth Sunday of Advent. They may have been used in a worship service that you attended today. You may wish to explore the readings using different translations and having different readers. Notice the mention of Bethlehem, the preparations for birth, and the changes for the world that are anticipated.

Candle Lighting

Light four candles on the Advent wreath. If you have not placed a white candle in the middle of the wreath, this is a good time to place one there in anticipation of lighting it on Christmas Eve or Christmas Day and for the twelve days of Christmas.

Prayer: *May the light from these candles illuminate the way to Bethlehem, where we will kneel in wide-eyed wonder and offer prayers of blessing and thanks. Companion God, go with us this week as we approach the manger with open hearts.*

Prayers

Lift up any joys or concerns in a time of prayer.

One pattern of sharing encourages the person praying to say, "This is my prayer" after mentioning an intention for a person or situation. Others then may respond, "This is our prayer."

You are encouraged to use this pattern or discover a pattern that works for you.

A Look Ahead

Before concluding your prayers around the Advent wreath, look briefly at your coming week. Notice any events, meetings, or activities that you may want to hold in prayer as part of your daily reading and reflection.

Make plans for special Christmas Eve or Christmas Day services. Arrange your readings for the week to include Christmas if it occurs this week. Look ahead at the suggested activities for the weekend in preparation for Christmas Day.

Day One

A Strange Way to Save the World

I love to sing Christmas carols. I try not to sing any until Christmas Eve, though I do listen to all kinds of Christmas music throughout Advent. One Advent, the choir soloist and I decided to add a contemporary song to our Christmas Eve celebration, one she would sing as special music. We sing plenty of traditional carols but sometimes one of the new songs wheedles its way into our library.

In 1993, Dave Clark, Mark Harris, and Don Koch wrote a song titled, "A Strange Way to Save the World." The song questions why God chose a baby, a simple carpenter, and an ordinary girl to bring the Savior into the world. The song is sung from Joseph's perspective and asks the haunting questions, *Why me? Why her? Why here? Why a baby?* Indeed, it is a strange way to save the world.

I am glad the song is still popular and that the juxtaposition is still relevant. If we were trying to change the world, would we have started with a baby? Certainly a study committee, fully-funded, would find a better way. For an event this momentous, we need:

a committee with bright minds and powerful people who can get things done; whiteboards, newsprint, and computers to make lists and calculate success rates; a listing of resources, tools, and maybe even weapons to make it happen. We would want strategy, funding, and a whole media campaign, for sure.

But a baby?

If we were trying to stir up Christians to remember, would we have picked Francis, his donkey, and a manger with straw to start a worldwide way to remember and celebrate? Yet, for Francis, the Incarnation confirms the dignity of women and men. God created humans in God's own image and then chose to be human, in all the fullness of body and soul and with the limits of the human condition. The Babe in Bethlehem had a profound impact on Francis.

God takes a long view. Starting with a baby means this is a lifelong project. Maybe the poor shepherds will get a glimpse of the One who comes to be with the forgotten and oppressed. Maybe the magi, strangers, and foreigners will see the hope for a new world order and come, kneel, and find welcome.

I am glad for the old familiar carols, but every once in a while it is wonderful to find one that stirs up a new way to think of the miracle of Christmas.

Ponder

If possible, find a way to listen to "A Strange Way to Save the World." Thankfully, many artists have recorded it since its composition. What line or verse speaks to you?

God takes the long view. How has God been at work in your life? Take some time for reflection. Draw a chart or a map of significant moments on your spiritual journey.

Perhaps in the new year you will want to schedule time to meet with a spiritual director who is gifted in helping you see and pay attention to the movements of the Spirit in your life. Spiritual Direction International is an organization I belong to. It has a listing of spiritual directors around the world. (Visit sdiworld.org.)

Light four Advent candles.

Pray

Surprising God, thank you for choosing to be with us as a child who needs our care and tenderness in an often harsh world. Thank you for taking the long view and thank you for your persistent work to bend the world toward compassion and justice. Thank you for your humble beginnings, showing us that we don't need to look too high or too far to find your presence in the ordinary, the humble, the poor, or the beautiful. Thank you that your love reaches us again and again. Amen.

Day Two

Special Night, Silent Night

As a pastor, Christmas Eve day was a busy workday with final planning for a Christmas Eve service for families and children. Sometimes there was a children's pageant, which required a final rehearsal or early arrival to get the church open and the costumes on. When we did not have a pageant or children's choir or readings, I often read or created a special children's story that took the place of a sermon. The festive service concluded with lighting candles and singing "Silent Night," a holy moment even for the little ones.

Before the later service (thankfully not a midnight service for our young children), we were able to have a meal at home before I headed back to church to pick up used candles, change the bulletins, and check with the choir and other participants in the "adult" service. It was a long, full, and good day.

Even in the midst of leading worship, there were moments of awe and wonder. A song the choir sang, a line or verse from the liturgy or scripture reading, the spread of candlelight through the sanctuary touched my spirit. When I moved from local congregation pastoring to retreat ministry and did not have church worship responsibilities, the number of grace-filled moments swelled as I sat in the pew. Singing the carols in a large church with all the stops pulled out on the organ was way different from my former sanctuary that seated less than one hundred. Hundreds of candles lit from the main floor to the balconies contrasted greatly with the small churches I previously served that didn't even have balconies.

Like Saint Francis, I was inspired by the birth story and wrote some of my favorite prayers and spirit-inspired lines used in worship. I am still touched by the questions and the affirmations in this Christmas Eve prayer:

> *Can one night make a difference? Can one star outshine all others? Can one Child shake up the world? Yes, a thousand times, yes!*
>
> *Was ever there such a night, when stars shone bright, when angels formed a heavenly chorus and shepherds quaked? Was ever there such a birth, when a Baby's cry meant that God is now here? Was ever there a moment like now, when we let the majesty and simplicity of the story touch our hearts, when we draw closer to family and God, when we sing with deep feeling and overflowing joy? Oh, this is the night, this is the night.*
>
> *Oh, that our tongues were like bells to ring out the joy and that our hands were like drums to sound out the beat of new*

*life. Oh, that our voices sounded like the heavenly choir
and that our hearts could hold the wonder of it all. Oh, that
our knees were strong enough to kneel forever in awe and
that our eyes could open wide enough to see glory shining in
every star and in every person. Amen.*[1]

I like to think that Saint Francis would have joined in and said,
"Yes, a thousand times, yes."

A chapel now encompasses the stone altar that Francis used in
the twelfth century, with a larger church nearby. I will travel there
and see the place and feel the holy surroundings that stirred the
little man of God to begin a tradition of seeing and experiencing
something of the wonder of a God who bends down to embrace
who we are.

Whether you travel to Greccio in Italy or not, you can feel
the wonder of Christmas Eve in large churches and small, with a
few candles or none, with trumpets and organ or simply guitar and
piano, and always with voices raised in praise.

Ponder

Recall a memory you have of a Christmas Eve service that touched
your heart. Share the memory with a friend or family member.

What prayer would you write this evening?

Find a line from a favorite Christmas carol and let it be the start
of your prayer.

Light four Advent candles and the white candle if you have
used one in your Advent wreath.

Pray

*Holy Child, bring light into the shadows of our lives and the darkness of
our world. Open us to hope that radiates from the manger. Open us to
joy that arrives in angel songs. Open us to peace that resides in Mary's*

gaze and Joseph's care. Surprise us in wintry darkness with gifts of love,
unwrapped and present in every person, every prayer, and every song.
Soften our hearts to the wonder of this holy night.

Loving God, Holy Child, surprise us again and again with peace,
bless us with joy, and send us forward to love and serve. Amen.

Day Three

Welcome Baby Jesus

Merry Christmas! The day long expected is finally here. Rejoice, shout for joy, and give thanks. Wish everyone a Merry Christmas!

When I was a young boy, our five-member family lived in a two-story house, with the three bedrooms and one bathroom all on the second floor. On Christmas morning, with anticipation building, our parents made my brother, sister, and me wait so we could go downstairs together. One year, my sister—the youngest of us—broke the rule and sprinted down before the rest of us. My parents called her back and, as she came racing up the stairs, my brother and I yelled, "Don't tell!" because we knew a few of the gifts were not wrapped. She looked at us and said, "Hockey sticks." We were so disappointed. She hadn't seen her gifts but managed to spoil the surprise for my brother and me. Still, we did enjoy those hockey sticks, which were much better than the previous homemade ones, with their nails that sent me to the hospital for stitches after I sustained a cut in a face-off. We tell the hockey sticks story often and have a good laugh.

When my wife and I had children, we recognized the great anticipation our children experienced for both wrapped and unwrapped gifts. Our family found a way to remind us that we were celebrating the birth of Jesus. Before we opened gifts, we went around to each baby in every crèche set and said, "Welcome, Baby Jesus!" The ritual was fun, and it gave us a reason to look at the international flavor around us on this holy morning. Now our children are grown, and we have many more crèche sets than we did when they were small. Still, "Welcome, Baby Jesus!" is our Christmas morning tradition.

One year, while I served as a retreat director and did not have Sunday or Christmas responsibilities, our family took a vacation over Christmas and New Year to Portugal. We each carried a few gifts in our luggage so we could celebrate gift giving as a family. When we woke on Christmas morning, we put a few wrapped presents on a makeshift table. But before we could sit to give and receive, our grown children said we had to do the ritual. My wife and I quizzically looked at them. They got out a computer and proceeded to open a document that had pictures of all the crèche sets from our home. We gathered around the computer, looked at the images, and said, "Welcome, Baby Jesus!" It was one of the most special moments of our trip.

Ponder

What Christmas memories do you have, especially memories of how your family celebrates the birth of Christ on Christmas Day?

Which Christmas carol causes you to tear up? Make sure you play that carol or sing that carol today.

What would it mean for you to welcome Baby Jesus into your life every day? What ritual would center you in that amazing gift every day?

Light the white candle or another candle in honor of the birth of Christ.

Pray

To us, watchful and waiting, a gift has been slipped into our midst—a tiny Child, born in a manger.

A gift of peace to troubled souls and dangerous streets.

A gift of joy to sad hearts and cautious lives.

A gift of hope to wearied brows and oppressed peoples.

A tiny Baby meant for us in our fractured world and in our hectic and stressed lives.

Holy One, open our hearts to receive, our hands to care, and our voices to praise on this most holy and glorious day. Amen.

Day Four

Boxing Day

The first Christmas I spent in Manchester, England, as part of my seminary education some years ago, I learned that not everyone celebrates Christmas in the same way. On one level, I knew this from reading and from people's stories, but it is quite different to experience it.

I was used to Christmas Eve worship services, carols, and candlelight. In my experience in England, Christmas Eve was more family-oriented, and, thankfully, a church family invited me to join them for dinner at a restaurant and then an evening of gift giving. Christmas Day in the Manchester church was a day for worship and service. A Christmas morning celebration began the day, though I don't remember if we sang *Silent Night*. Following the worship service, we all moved quickly to the church hall to finish preparing and then serving a free meal to the poor and disabled in the area. Before serving dessert with lots of British tea, the energetic church crew provided entertainment, including a Christmas carol sing-along. It was late in the afternoon before we cleaned up. I was worn out, but happy for a day of praise and service. Thankfully, we retired to one family's home for refreshments, stories, and memories from the day.

Next was Boxing Day, the day after Christmas, which has nothing to do with the sport of boxing or with the plan to recycle boxes after gift giving. The day exists to remember those who serve you throughout the year with a gift—a box of something. It is a day to remember the letter carrier, the milk deliverer (yes, I had milk in small glass bottles delivered to my door each day), the corner green grocer who provided my fresh vegetables, and the newspaper seller where I stopped to buy a paper on my way to the church. I can't remember if I gave something to the owner of the "chippy" where I purchased fish and chips several times a week. Boxing Day is a most British custom of remembering those who serve, though it probably has roots in an aristocratic era when boxes were given to servants and employees of the estate who had the day off after a long day of serving during the big Christmas feasts. Think *Downton Abbey*.

Boxing Day may also have roots in the tradition of churches in the United Kingdom opening the alms box, the collection box for the poor kept in church. These boxes were traditionally opened on Boxing Day and the money distributed to the poor.

Though it is still a national holiday in the United Kingdom, some of the traditions of gift giving to those who serve have lessened as milk is no longer delivered, corner stores have disappeared, and families have turned their attention to other activities.

The day after Christmas is also called the Feast of St. Stephen, likely named for the first martyr in the early church as recorded in Acts chapters 6 and 7. Stephen was the first Deacon of the early church and responsible for caring for the poor, another link to the tradition of Boxing Day.

For several reasons, the day after Christmas is a good day to think of others. Francis wrote a "Letter to the Faithful" around 1220 filled with encouragement to remember others. "And let us love our neighbors as our selves. And if anyone does not want to love them as himself, let him at least not do them any harm, but let him do good. . . . Let us, therefore, have charity and humility and give alms because it washes the stains from our souls."[2]

Ponder

How will you celebrate this second day of Christmas? How might it be a day to practice compassion for those who are less fortunate?

Light the Christ candle and continue to give thanks that God cares for all of creation.

Pray

Holy One, Source of Everlasting Joy, how happy we are to continue celebrating Christmas, when the sun shone brighter and the world was bathed in holy light, when our eyes twinkle at candlelight and Christmas tree lights, when the songs we sing pushed back the darkness and troubles of the world, and when the world bowed on bended knee to adore the newborn Savior.

Holy One, Source of Everlasting Joy, how blessed are we to live in the light and hope and love of your humble birth. How blessed it is to serve others in need. Amen.

Day Five

Praising God for the Gift of Jesus

Music stirs feelings and can lift our mood. Christmas songs point us to Bethlehem, to God who bends low to journey with us. Santa songs leave me cold, but hymns and carols warm my heart.

Many people know that Francis composed the Canticle to Brother Sun, extolling the virtues of Brother Sun, Sister Moon and Stars, Brothers Wind and Air, Sister Water, Brother Fire, Sister Earth, and finally Sister Death.[3] All creation praises God.

Less well-known is his "Praises of God," which he wrote later in life and after spending time with the Muslims who have a prayer with ninety-nine names or attributes of God. Francis wrote it to encourage Brother Leo. This week it can carry our joy for the God who gives us Jesus to be with us, and for whom we love and care.

> You are holy, Lord, the only God,
> and your deeds are wonderful.
> You are strong.
> You are great. You are the Most High,
> You are almighty.
> You, Holy Father, are King of heaven and earth.
> You are Three and One,
> Lord God, all good.
> You are Good, all Good, supreme Good,
> Lord God, living and true.
> You are love,
> You are wisdom.
> You are humility, you are endurance.
> You are rest, you are peace.
> You are joy and gladness.
> You are justice and moderation.

You are all our riches, and you suffice for us.
You are beauty.
    You are gentleness.
    You are our protector, you are our guardian and
    defender.
    You are courage.
    You are our heaven and our hope.
You are our faith,
    Our great consolation.
    You are our eternal life, great and wonderful Lord,
    God almighty,
    Merciful Saviour.[4]

Ponder

Think of the significance of God coming in flesh to be one with us
and write your own praises of God.

Pray

*Amazing God, tender Child, we offer you our words brimming with
joy. We offer you our hands ready to lift up the fallen and to preserve
creation. We offer our feet to walk alongside those in need. We offer you
our hearts that we may be persistent in love and faithful in caring.*

Light the Christ Candle if you have not already done so.

Weekend Activity

As Christmas draws to a close, review any preparation that you still
need, including ways that you can help others celebrate the birth
of the One to whom the angels sing, "Glory to the newborn King."

Is there someplace that will be serving a Christmas meal to the
homeless or needy or new immigrants where you could volunteer?

Are there college students (often international students) who have no place to go for Christmas once the dorms close? Could you welcome one or several for a day or a meal?

Is there someone to whom you could offer a ride to a Christmas Eve service? As far as I know, my grandmother never drove. But thinking back I see the kindness of my father who arranged to pick up Grandma for church and for special services. She may not have driven, but she made a special scalloped potato dish enjoyed by many for church potluck suppers.

If Christmas has already arrived, consider ways that you could help a neighbor that needs assistance during this Christmas season. Again, I remember my mother baking an extra pie or making an extra plate of cookies to take to the neighbors. As a youth, I resented the loss of a pie or cookies. Now I look back with gratitude for the model of kindness that touched lives and made our street a caring neighborhood.

Pray

Coming God, soon and even now, we witness
    the Birth of hope,
    the cradle of wonder
    the bud of peace
    the sliver of starlight
    the chorus of joy.
We are grateful. We rejoice. We twirl with delight.

Or,

Use a favorite Christmas carol as your prayer. What carol do you know by heart? Prayerfully sing or say at least one verse.

✳ FIFTH WEEK ✳

Challenges and Resolutions

Introduction

What a shift from last week, from *are we there yet?* to *is it already over?* Of course, the answer is *no*. This is just the beginning of living into the reminder and the celebration that God is with us. God is with us as we enter into a new year and as we set intentions or resolutions to be different, to live better, to let go of the past, and to trust the future by living fully aware of the present.

This week we also begin into shift to the season of Epiphany, the reality that God is alive in all places and with all people if we have the eyes to see the many ways God appears.

This is also the last week of these written meditations, but hopefully not the last days for you to have a daily discipline of prayer, reading, and reflection. There are many resources available for you to use to continue to create time for centering yourself in the love and guidance of God. *The Upper Room Daily Devotional Guide* and Upper Room *Disciplines* are two key resources for you. And I have written a book called *Openings: A Daybook of Saints, Sages, Psalms and Prayer Practices* that you might like to check out.

You may want to pray this prayer for the beginning of the week. Let it inspire your words and prayers.

> *Wonderful Counselor, Mighty God, Holy Lover, journey with*
>   *us all year.*
> *Walk with us step by step,*
> *hold us in the darkness,*
> *shelter us in the storms,*
> *guide us among the many paths,*
> *push us when the going is rough,*
> *encourage us up the steep climbs,*
> *skip with us through the still meadows*
> *and sit with us by quiet streams.*
> *Companion God, one day at a time, into your new day and*
>   *new year may we be ready to go. Amen.*

Depending on when you are reading this study, you may want to alter the readings to match up with New Year's Eve, New Year's Day, and Epiphany.

Consider participating in a New Year's Eve Watch Night service or a Sunday worship service that uses John Wesley's Covenant Prayer.

First Sunday after Christmas Day

If your Advent wreath is still available, Light the Christ candle.

Centering Time

Take a few deep breaths. Breathe in peace with each inhale. Breathe out worry with each exhale. Breathe in love, let go of hate.

Pray

Holy One, thank you for the gift of yourself. Thank you for trusting us with your precious Child, and forgive us for not caring for the young, for distrusting people who are different, for choosing violence to solve problems, for looking down on the poor, and for abusing creation. Renew our compassion and care this Christmas and let each nativity set stir our hearts and kindle our joy. Amen.

Reading

Choose from Psalm 148; Colossians 3:12-17; Luke 2:41-52; or Matthew 2:13-23.

These are lessons often used on the Sunday after Christmas Day. They may have been used in a worship service that you attended today. You may wish to explore the readings using different translations and having different readers read them aloud.

Prayers

Lift up any joys or concerns in a time of prayer.

One pattern of sharing encourages the person praying to say, "This is my prayer" after mentioning an intention for a person or situation. Others then may respond, "This is our prayer."

Use this pattern or discover a pattern that works for you.

Give thanks for this journey and for those who have joined you. Consider whether you wish to continue meeting and what resources you might use. Encourage one another to continue with the daily meditations that take you to Epiphany.

Day One

The 12 Days of Christmas

Like many Advent and Christmas traditions, the song, "The Twelve Days of Christmas" has differing interpretations, layers of meaning, and a questionable history. Some believe it is a folkloric song, a children's nonsense song with secular origins that is mostly about birds.

Others suggest that it is a song of hidden theological meaning dating back to the sixteenth century religious wars in England. In this Christian interpretation, the song contains references to biblical and church images used to instruct Roman Catholic youth, even as the Anglican rulers outlawed the Roman Catholic Church. The "true love" that gives gifts on each of the twelve days is not some earthly suitor, but it is God who gives Jesus, the mother hen or partridge who lays down her life for her children.

The other symbols of the Christian faith are usually listed as follows:

- 2 turtle doves = the Hebrew scriptures and New Testament
- 3 french hens = faith, hope, and charity—the theological virtues
- 4 calling birds = the four Gospels or the Four Evangelists
- 5 golden rings = the first five books of the Hebrew scriptures
- 6 geese a-laying = the six days of Creation
- 7 swans a-swimming = the seven days of Creation, or seven gifts of the Holy Spirit
- 8 maids a-milking = the eight Beatitudes
- 9 ladies dancing = the nine fruits of the Spirit
- 10 lords a-leaping = the Ten Commandments
- 11 pipers piping = the eleven faithful disciples

- 12 drummers drumming = the twelve points of doctrine in the Apostles Creed

This accounting has made listening to the "The 12 Days of Christmas," with its many repeating refrains, more tolerable for me; but some church historians have pointed out apparent historical and logical discrepancies. For example, both Anglicans and Catholics would agree on the interpretations of the "hidden meanings," which leads to no distinctions worthy of punishment. As a tool for memorizing a catechism, there is no content in this song. Though the Gospels do have some references to Jesus longing to gather the people as a mother hen, it is hard to imagine the theologians from the sixteenth century leading the way in exploring feminine images for Jesus or God.

Leaving the song aside, both the Western and Eastern Church (now known as the Orthodox branch) have celebrated the twelve days between Christmas and Epiphany, Epiphany being the traditional day celebrating the coming of the magi or wise men. Advent was the season of preparation with its four Sundays, followed by twelve days to celebrate the wonderful gift of God becoming human and dwelling with us. I am not sure if the popular song helps us, but it has firmly planted the twelve days of Christmas in our minds.

Ponder

How are you keeping Christmas alive during the twelve days?

What tools do you use to keep elements of the faith in your memory?

Can you name the Beatitudes or the fruits of the spirit? Might these be guides that you would want to commit to memory? Henri Nouwen once wrote an article entitled, "What do you know by heart?" I don't remember the whole article, but the title has stuck with me and invited me to memorize selected verses of scripture.

Light the Christ candle sometime during the day or evening.

Pray

God of songs and silence, poetry and dance, thank you for weaving your way into our world, into our voices, into our memories. Thank you for this Christmas season, these twelve days, so rich with song and melody. Help us to keep singing and to keep Christmas in our hearts and on our lips.

Remind us that you are the Great Lover who gives us the gift of your own presence every day. Amen.

Day Two

New Year's Eve

One year I was invited to a different kind of New Year's Eve party. Besides the normal potluck dish to share at a friend's house, we were encouraged to bring our journals and openness to a time of silence. After meeting one another, we had a wonderful dinner and conversation as people looked for common connections. We shared stories of how we each knew someone in the group. We found much in common, from a trip to Turkey, to living on the same coast at one time, to leading spirituality retreats.

Following dinner, the host gave us a list of questions and invited us to take an hour of silence to reflect about the past year and our hopes for the year to come. We each found a cozy space in the home and entered into the reflections, sometimes using the questions and sometimes simply recalling experiences of the year. The questions were along these lines:

> What was your greatest joy in the year? Do you have any regrets or things you would like to do over? How have you grown as a person, employee, neighbor, or church member? Did you find a scripture passage that became a guiding light for you this year? In the new year, is there a special inward or outward work you would like to accomplish?

And many more questions.

Coming back together, we were invited to share thoughts or insights that came from the time of reflection. Despite not knowing some persons very well, the exercise created a holy space, and the sharing was rich and deep.

We did not stay until midnight, but the drive home maintained a peace and a joy better than a big gathering or a loud party. It remains a most memorable New Year's Eve party.

Ponder

What in the past year was life-affirming? What was life-draining?

Are there any persons to whom you need to reach out for forgiveness or to make amends?

What call from God are you sensing for the New Year? Are there any transitions or changes that you anticipate or need to make?

Who are the companions that travel with you? Who are the ones who would search for you if you were lost?

Pray

May there always be stars to guide you and a smooth road for you to travel. May you know a thousand blessings each day. May God give

you hope each morning and peace at each evening's rest. May God walk
beside you now and always.

Day Three

New Year

How shall we enter the new year? For most of us, it is not an either/
or, black/white, this road/that road clear choice. We enter filled with
great expectations and a touch of worry. We enter with a bundle of
hope and a measure of doubt; a bold new plan and a few details not
yet conceived. We are a mixture of past and future, abundant joy
and lingering sorrow. We strive to be fully alive and awake each day
without any guarantees. Except, we do not travel alone.

Christmas is the sign and the promise that God has bent low to
be with us. From lowly shepherds to foreign travelers, God comes
and dwells with them and with us.

I don't remember any particular traditions in our family about
New Year's Day except watching football. Still, my wife thinks
we should have black-eyed peas, despite not really being from the
South. The tradition has something to do with good luck and the
Internet has multiple meanings about why black-eyed peas became
associated with New Year's Day.

The tradition may come from Jews eating black-eyed peas on
Rosh Hashanah, the Jewish New Year. In the South, the humble
peas were mixed with greens, symbolizing money and served with
cornbread, hence the expression, "Peas for pennies, greens for dol-
lars, and cornbread for gold." Others thought that if you ate simply and poorly on New Year's Day, you would eat "fat" the rest of
the year.

So we joyfully eat black-eyed peas and greens on New Year's Day and think about the coming days filled with a variety of experiences from simple day-to-day tasks to vacation time and maybe a trip. A whole year awaits, and we have some fuel to get us going.

Ponder

What new year traditions do you recall from the past, or what New Year's Day traditions do you still carry out?

What spiritual practices do you want to start or continue to keep you fully alive and awake?

Pray

Creative God, you make all things new and you hold out a new day and a new year for us. Thank you.

Yet how often we squander the opportunities, miss the invitations, ignore the possibilities. We let doubts overtake us and we let fears overwhelm us. You offer us new dreams, yet we succumb to familiar scripts. You offer us new risks, but we settle for safe paths.

Creative God, send your angels to sing us songs of hope on dark and silent nights. Fill us with the joy of living and the spirit of giving as we enter the new year. Walk with us, guide us, and direct us in the company of the Spirit. Amen.

Day Four

Resolutions

The average American abandons his or her New Year's resolutions in about six weeks. Or about the time that the crowded gym classes return to their normal size. Breaking our resolutions keep comedians employed for the start of a new year, and sales of exercise machines climb dramatically from December to January.

Most resolutions are about self-care, with losing weight and improving health usually topping the list. Getting closer to God or being kinder to others or working for justice are further down the list, if on the list at all. Yet, our best intentions often fall short of our goals.

We often fall short because our new year intentions depend so much on our willpower and our efforts without being grounded on, rooted in, or supported by the pull and push of the Spirit. A friend of mine says willpower is an exhaustible resource; it just takes too much effort to keep going. The intention of getting more exercise is good, yet how does it fit into a holistic plan for caring for God's temple, the body? Our willpower can only get us so far. God's care and nudges can sustain us over the long haul.

Further, I have discovered that new practices, whether about good health or growing spiritually, need to be folded into our daily patterns. Our intentions have to become practices and habits; and that takes faithful effort, the support of a community or family or friends, and deliberate planning and repetition. There is truth to the old story about a traveler asking a New Yorker how to get to Carnegie Hall and receiving the reply, "Practice, practice, practice."

Charles Duhigg, in his book *The Power of Habit*, emphasizes the importance of keystone habits, or habits that create momentum to establish other positive habits in your life. Exercise is one of those keystone habits that results in better health, good eating habits, and personal productivity. I believe prayer is another keystone habit that enables other spiritual practices and provides centering to our day and activities.

As I have offered spiritual direction to people over the years, people have asked how to develop a better prayer life with the hope that I had a magic or simple solution. There are many practices or habits one could adopt, like befriending silence, walking a labyrinth, *lectio divina*, centering prayer, keeping a journal, or working in a soup kitchen. Yet the first questions are really, "What is your heart's desire? What is your longing?" Can we recognize our response to God's extravagant love as the Spirit's gentle nudge and soft push to develop practices of openness, receptivity, and gratitude? Can we thank God for planting the desire in us and trust that God will help us stay on the path? God leads us beside still waters and along right paths according the psalmist in Psalm 23. Can we deeply trust and follow the One who leads us?

First comes the intention, the strong desire, and the trust that God goes with us; then follows the particular ways and habits of enacting our response to a loving God. Those intentions become habits, even keystone habits and lifelong companions, keeping us awake and open to the amazing love of God.

As you enter the new year, may this prayer from Saint Francis be a companion and keep you open to guidance from the Holy One:

Most High, glorious God,
enlighten the darkness of my heart
and give me true faith, certain hope,
and perfect charity, sense, and knowledge, Lord,
that I may carry out your holy and true command.[1]

This prayer has also become a popular song from the Franciscan brother, John Michael Talbot, titled, "A Prayer for Guidance" on his album *Troubadour of the Great King*. I sing it to myself most mornings as I head to work.

Ponder

What is your strongest desire for the new year? What spiritual practice or service would you like to deepen or restore?

How do you plan to rest beside still waters this year?

What new paths might God be calling you to follow?

Pray

God of new beginnings, take us into this new year with hope and healing. Let us keep our vows and commitments to make this a better world. Too often, we plan the party but not the protest, we enjoy the harvest but forget the workers, and we count our blessings but neglect to share them with others.

Open our lives to the in-breaking of your new reign, seen by shepherds and magi, and proclaimed again in this new year.

Child of promise and peace, love us into the new year and through each day. Amen.

Day Five

Let Go, Hold On

I have a new granddaughter and I recently gave her a bottle of breast milk while her mother was at work. As I held her and we looked at one another, she reached out and grabbed my finger. I think, given her young age, it was not coordinated intention, but an accidental touch. Regardless, once she found my finger, she held on.

As we begin the new year, we look back to see the things we want to hold, things we want to keep in our memory bank. The prophets of ancient Israel frequently called the people to remember the actions of God. "I brought you out of Egypt; I rescued you from slavery; I sent Moses, Aaron and Miriam to lead you. . . . Remember these things and you will realize what I did in order to save you" (Mic. 6:4-5, GNT).

I have found it helpful to create a spiritual autobiography or a faith journey timeline to look back at the highs and lows of my spiritual journey and remember the ways that God has been with me. Like the contemporary gospel hymn says, God has been there, through it all. "Through it all, through it all, I've learned to trust in Jesus, I've learned to trust in God."[2] Hold on to the assurance that God is with us. Hold on to the signs from the past year that give hope and promise.

Of course, we can get stuck in the past, hanging on to old hurts and slights, old wounds and disappointments, abuses and disasters. The prophets want us to remember the faithfulness of God in the past but not to linger there. "Do not cling to events of the past or dwell on what happened long ago. Watch for the new thing I am going to do. It is happening already—you can see it now. I will make a road through the wilderness and give you streams of water there" (Isa. 43:18-19, GNT). Or in the New Revised Standard Version translation, "I am about to do a new thing; now it springs forth, do you not perceive it?"

God is moving into this new year with you and it is filled with untold wonders and experiences. How can we let go of old experiences and old expectations and be open to the new ways God will be with us?

When I began to wonder about the next stages in ministry, I went on a retreat. As part of the daylong retreat, the leader invited us to take a Bible verse from a basket. I don't know how she selected the verses and I don't know if they were all the same, but I do know that the verse I randomly selected was Isaiah 43:18-19. In the midst of my questions and doubts, in the midst of holding on and anticipating letting go, the words from Isaiah became a touchstone for me in a season of discernment. God will make a way in the wilderness of wonderings and questions and sleepless nights and worry. God will provide streams of new possibilities and encouragement and job opportunities in the desert of rejections and "thanks but no thanks."

A new year is unfolding. One of my friends translates a verse from Psalm 118 from past tense to present tense. "This the day the LORD *is making*. Let us rejoice and give thanks" (Ps. 118: 24, AP). It is a good verse to use this day and every day of this new year.

Ponder

What would your spiritual autobiography look like? Can you draw a timeline or list significant events in each decade of your life? Is there someone with whom you could share this recording and together give thanks?

What scripture verse is a touchstone for you? Is there a verse that you want to have as your guide for this new year?

Pray

God of the journey, weave these days of the Christmas season into the turning of the calendar page. Remind us that Christmas joy is loose in the world, love is lodged in hearts, and peace is still our fervent hope. Though the presents are all unwrapped, the batteries run down, and family members have returned home, you are calling us to live like parents of new born babies, living with tender compassion, gentle care, and overflowing love—for ourselves, for our neighbors, for our earth, and for our world. Be with us this day, throughout this new year, and always. Amen.

Day Six

Encouragement

We began this Advent and Christmas journey with the companionship of Saint Francis, the little man of God, who was so in love with the Incarnation that he wanted the world to see Jesus and know the God who bent low to complete creation.

Saint Francis continues as one of the best known and most popular saints in the world and now, with a pope who bears his name, Saint Francis is even more well-known. The world is blessed by this follower of Jesus who loved creation, embraced simplicity, and lived peaceably with all.

Although I love the story of the living nativity, his preaching to the birds, and the taming of the wolf at Grubbio, the story of Francis's visit with Sultan Malik al-Kamil in 1219 during the Crusades is the one that challenges and encourages me. (See Third Week: Day Four.) Though we don't know what transpired between them, we do know that Francis walked out of the meeting alive and with a new respect for people who believed in God, even if outside the bounds of Christianity.

When Francis authored *The Rule*, a guide and admonition for how the brothers who followed his teachings were to live as disciples of Jesus and commit to poverty and peacemaking, he included a chapter of instructions for friars living between Muslims and other non-Christians. He told the brothers to respect their beliefs, religion, and culture and to only preach when circumstances permitted. They were to live as peacemakers, a radically different approach in the time of the Crusades, a time when the power of the sword was used more often than the power of the Spirit. One writer puts this important contribution of Francis this way: "Francis has much to say today to those who are interested in interreligious dialogue . . . after all, he invented it."[3] It is no surprise or accident that we attribute the prayer, "Lord, make me an instrument of your peace" to Saint Francis.

Francis not only opened our eyes to see the humble Babe of Bethlehem and the God who bends low to be with us, but the life and witness of Saint Francis continues to offer guidance for living faithfully in our often troubled and fearful world.

Here are two final words from Saint Francis:

We should not be wise and prudent according to worldly standards, but rather we should be simple, humble, and pure. We should never desire to be above others, but rather we should be servants, and subject for the Lord's sake to every kind of authority. Upon all who do these things and endure to the end will rest the Spirit of the Lord. . . .[4]

And, his final word to the brothers and to us, "I have done what is mine; may Christ teach you yours."[5]

Ponder

What word of encouragement do you take for this coming year?

Is there a hymn or song or prayer or poem that you want to be your companion for the whole year?

Pray

Holy One, thank you for the gift of your servant Francis and the way he lived simply and prayerfully a life of devotion. May we also walk lightly and humbly on the earth, caring gently for all creation and living in peace with all persons. Amen.

Weekend Activity

This could be a good weekend to make some preparations for Epiphany, a feast day that is seldom celebrated but is the culmination of the twelve days of Christmas. Our family used to prepare a display of the three magi that would remain on our dinner table for the Sundays until Lent began. We also would hang stars in the house to help us remember the star that guided the magi or kings to the manger. Adding white lights to outside decorations or trees would be another bright sign to guide the way of the magi.

What other Epiphany symbols could you add to your home?

Epiphany

On Epiphany (January 6), the celebration of Christmas comes to an end with the visit of the magi to the Christ child. When children (and adults, too) are asked about the story, they often tell you about three kings who rode camels to see the Baby in a manger. From legend, songs, and pageants, we have these images, but the writer of Matthew does not add these details.

We do not know how many people made the trip, but we assume that three gifts (gold, frankincense, and myrrh) meant that there were three individuals. We are told they are wise or magi, which usually means from the learned class in an ancient country in the East. Perhaps they rode camels and perhaps they were astrologers. Matthew does not say, but he does write that they enter a house and see the Child with Mary. Tradition, not Matthew, has named the three and given them regions to represent: Melchior, Caspar, and Balthazar—representing Europe, Arabia, and Africa respectively, traveling by horse, camel, and elephant in order to present baby Jesus with three symbolic gifts.

The context of the story introduces us to a ruthless and jealous King Herod, and to priests who knew of the scriptures about a ruler who would come from Bethlehem, but they missed the star. We also learn of the tragic consequences that come when the powerful are threatened and have means to impose death on the powerless.

Epiphany, a word meaning manifestation, ushers us into a season when we look at the way God has entered the world, reaching out to all nations and all peoples. From the poor shepherds to the magi from the East, God beckons. During the Sundays after the Epiphany, the common lectionary (a list of readings for each Sunday of the year on a three-year cycle) celebrates the visit of the magi, the baptism of Jesus, and the turning of water into wine at the wedding feast of Cana. Each of these stories brings the presence of God into our world.

Epiphany is celebrated in different ways around the world. Orthodox Christians traditionally have their homes blessed with holy water on or around this day. In Latin America, Epiphany—or Three Kings Day—is the day for giving gifts in honor of the wise visitors of the East and for eating Rosca de Reyes (King's Ring), a sweet bread shaped like a wreath with candied fruit on top and a figurine of a baby Jesus baked inside.

In Ethiopia, pilgrims from all over the country converge on the ancient city of Aksum, where they bathe in a great reservoir of water that has been blessed by a priest.

Most churches in the United States celebrate Epiphany on the Sunday closest to January 6. Stars to guide the way, the color green, and stories of the international reach of God dominate the worship of the season.

Ponder

How do you celebrate the story of the magi?

What gifts can you give that would honor the Christ child and to whom can you give them?

What symbols can you place in your home to remind you to welcome strangers?

Pray

Holy One, place a star in our world and in our hearts and let us kneel in wonder, bringing the gift of our simple life for you to receive, bless, and empower. Fill us with your Spirit so we may reach out with your love to all those in need, regardless of their color or religion or language. Let this new year bring joy and healing, justice and peace. For us, for all. Amen.

Leader's Guide

Individual time for reading and reflecting can be enhanced and deepened by sharing with others. This Leader's Guide assumes individuals are spending time each day with the daily reading, particularly with the questions to ponder. Keeping a journal to record thoughts and questions each day is a great way to prepare for the weekly group sessions.

Groups should consider these hospitality matters in preparing to meet:

- purchase of books
- meeting place—comfortable setting with comfortable seating
- time—beginning time and ending time, flow of the meeting
- this guide has information for 90 minutes of directed sharing and activity
- meal, refreshments, and/or beverages
    Do you want to include any kind of food, snacks, or drinks? Would you want to hold the meetings in homes and with a meal or potluck? Who provides what and who cleans up?
- convener or alternating leadership to keep time as well as guide the discussion

Guideline for the Flow of the Gathering

- opening time of welcome, centering, meditation, and worship (15 minutes)
- reflecting on the readings and ponderings of the week (30 minutes)

- guided activity or experience—a mini retreat on the Advent journey (40 minutes)
- closing (5 minutes)

First Week Group Meeting

Take time to get acquainted. Besides sharing your name, share one memory you have of Advent or Christmas that touched your life. You might also share what drew you to the group.

Go over some guidelines or best practices for groups. Consider adding to this list:

- Speak from your own heart and own experience.
- Respect the experiences of others.
- Refrain from fixing or solving another's sharing.
- Ensure that all have the opportunity to share.
- Give space between sharing, and do not interrupt.

What would the group add to this list? Do you want to state a covenant for how your group will respect and care for one another?

You may also wish to take a photo of the group and share it via an online channel. Individuals can make prayer requests and the group will have a photo to help with remembering one another and the requests.

Opening Litany

(Read responsively or with each person saying a line.)

Advent is . . .

a pilgrimage of the soul.

a child's delight.

a journey to our own Bethlehem where something new waits to be born.

Advent is . . .

responding to a deep yearning.

going on a quest.

following a star to a place of wonder and joy.

Advent is . . .

bright lights and Christmas trees.

watching and anticipating.

waiting for a Baby's cry, the angels' song, and the whole world rejoicing.

Advent is our journey to the manger together.

Prayers

Share one-word prayers as you begin this journey together.

Sharing

What insights or questions arose for you from this week's readings? What was new, challenging, or life-giving from the readings, ponderings, or prayers?

Guided Activity

If the group plans to make an Advent wreath, some advanced preparation will be needed for the activity. Gather wreaths, candles, and evergreens.

If persons in the group have already made or already have Advent wreaths, extend the time of getting acquainted, making a group covenant, and sharing from the readings about Saint Francis and the living manger.

During the wreath-making activity, consider playing Advent/ Christmas instrumental music in the background to enhance the experience of creating Advent wreaths. Or, ask if the group would prefer silence or conversation.

Make an Advent wreath with four candles or make an Advent chain for yourself or for a family or community. Buy candles ahead of time and decide on the forms you will use to hold the candles. Be as creative as desired. Pine branches, if in your environment, are wonderful for covering the base of an Advent wreath.

Closing

Where can you make peace more visible in your life, in your home, in your neighborhood, in the world?

What other prayers would you like to share with the group? Include these five circles of care:

for my heart and soul,

for my home,

for my neighborhood or community,

for the earth,

for the world.

Holy One, make us instruments of your peace.

Second Week Group Meeting

Opening Litany

Advent is . . .
a thirsting for joy.
a hunger for peace.
a yearning for blessing.
a longing to kneel in wonder
and be lifted by angel songs
and softened by Baby sighs.
Advent is . . .
(Add your own thoughts.)

Prayers of Intercession

End your petition with "This is my prayer." The community responds with, "This is our prayer."

You may wish to use the list from last week as a way to extend the prayers of intercession:
for my heart and soul
for my home, family, and friends who need prayer
for my neighborhood or community
for the earth
for the world

Sharing

What insights or questions arose for you from this week's readings? What was new, challenging, or life-giving from the readings, ponderings, or prayers?

Guided Activity

Make your own crèche set in silence as the group listens to Christmas instrumentals. Each person can fashion one or maybe two nativity figures in the time allotted from clay or playdough or assorted building, craft, and play materials. Craft stores may have oven baking clay that hardens and lasts a bit longer. Have plenty of glue available if you use craft materials. Prepare the activity area with tables and chairs. Cover the table with paper if needed. At the conclusion, display the nativity figures. Do not be overly concerned if there are three Mary figurines and no shepherds. Each person may take home the figure he or she made.

Closing

Sing one verse of "Come Thou Long Expected Jesus" and pray this prayer:

Holy and Healing God, send us Jesus once again. We are still bound by sin and fear; our world still knows the grief of children dying from hunger and young ones dying in battle. Holy God, we long for an unending stream of hope and a deep reservoir of joy.

Holy and Just God, send us Jesus once again. Deliver us from petty squabbles, bruising busyness, hardened ears. Rule in our hearts with peace and reign in our world with compassion.

Holy and Loving God, send us Jesus once again. Let him be born in the words we say, revealed in the deeds we do, made alive in the care we extend. In every heart and nation, let peace reign. Amen.

Third Week Group Meeting

Opening Litany

Clear away the unnecessary.
Put aside the unimportant.
Lay down the unrealistic.
Cut the to-do lists in half.
Look for moments of silence.
Keep your eyes looking for a star,
Your hands ready to give,
Your knees ready to kneel,
Your voice ready to sing.
The Child will soon be born!

Prayers of Preparation

Where do you need to be ready?

After each sharing, the community responds: "Light for your path, strength for your journey, peace in your heart."

Sharing

What insights or questions arose for you from this week's readings? What was new, challenging, or life-giving from the readings, ponderings, or prayers?

Guided Activity

Create a Christmas prayer quilt—Draw a quilt (a book with quilt designs could help give ideas), and in each section, place a person for whom you are thankful or for whom you are praying. Color your quilt. There are many adult coloring books available, and they may have designs that you could use for the coloring activity.

For an additional activity, make stationery or cards to use next week for writing letters of encouragement. Provide nice paper, various ink stamps, and craft items. The group can decide on ways to fund this project.

Closing

Use the "Peace Prayer" of Saint Francis as a way to prepare to greet the Christ child in the midst of these last weeks of busyness:

Lord, make me an instrument of your peace:
where there is hatred, let me sow love;
where there is injury, pardon;
where there is doubt, faith;
where there is despair, hope;
where there is darkness, light;
where there is sadness, joy.

O divine Master, grant that I may not so much seek
to be consoled as to console,
to be understood as to understand,
to be loved as to love.
For it is in giving that we receive,
it is in pardoning that we are pardoned,
and it is in dying that we are born to eternal life.
Amen.

Fourth Week Group Meeting

Opening Litany

We are walking toward Bethlehem
Listening every step of the way for the sound of our name
that we have found favor with God
and something new is possible in and through us.
We are walking toward Bethlehem
sensing we are not alone
for angels are all around us
and saints are praying for us.
We are walking toward Bethlehem
A place of joy unleashed
Hope reborn
Peace rekindled.

Prayers

Try kneeling for a time of prayer. What gift would you bring to the
Child born in a manger? What gift do you offer the world?

Sharing

What insights or questions arose for you from this week's readings?
What was new, challenging, or life-giving from the readings, ponderings, or prayers?

Guided Activity

You will need to plan for this gathering.

Select persons or organizations that you could send a word of
thanks and encouragement. Look for the stories of people working
for peace, working to preserve some part of creation, or building
bridges to reconciliation. Find addresses ahead of time so you can

send the messages. Provide writing paper and envelopes or use the special cards or stationery that the group made last week.

Consider including a photo of the group.

Another option would be for the group to participate in a local service project, such as wrapping presents for a family in need or volunteering at a local toy or clothing drive. Are there ways your group could practice gift giving without expecting anything in return?

Closing

Share any insights you have received or commitments you have made as a result of this Advent study.

God of shepherds and kings, come near to us this week. Brush near with angels' wings and their songs of rejoicing. Open our eyes to wonder and your healing presence. May the familiar story shine new light on our paths and kindle holy love in our hearts.

God of shepherds and kings, thank you for journeying with us. Amen.

With a smile on your face and joy in your heart, share blessings with each other.

Fifth Week Group Meeting

Opening Litany

Arise, shine, for your Light has come.
Stand up, a new day is dawning
A new year is birthing
Fresh and clean
Arise, shine, for your Light has come.
Emmanuel, God is with us

On every path we take
No matter where we go
Arise, shine, for your Light has come.
And the stars still shine
Where Christ is present
And voices sing in praise.

Prayers for the New Year

What prayers do you have for the new year?
For yourselves?
For faith communities of which you are a part?
For the world and its people?
For those struggling, ill, oppressed?
For the earth?

Sharing

What insights or questions arose for you from this week's readings?
What was new, challenging, or life-giving from the readings, ponderings, or prayers?

Guided Activity

Advanced preparation will be necessary.

Plan on making Epiphany symbols for a dining room table or other place in the house to visually remind you of the days from Epiphany to Ash Wednesday and the beginning of Lent.

Here are some possibilities:

- Make three magi out of a variety of materials. One year our family used random pieces of wood from a carpenter friend. Our magi looked like they were surfing with long, flowing capes of various colors.

- Make stars that you can hang from doorways, arches, or chandeliers. Paper stars, origami stars, and starched string stars are some possibilities.
- It is also the season when we celebrate Jesus' baptism, Martin Luther King Jr.'s birthday, and Jesus' first miracle at a wedding. Consider images from those occasions that you could represent in your home. Display a water fountain? Write letters in support of peacemakers? Serve wedding cake at a meeting?

Closing

Share any resolutions you will make to be a more faithful follower of Jesus. Recall any encouragement you have received from the life of Saint Francis.

Offer blessings to one another.

NOTES

First Week

1. Thomas of Celano, *The Saint: The Writings of Francis Assisi*, Francis of Assisi: Early Documents, vol. 1, eds. Regis J. Armstrong, J.A Wayne Hellman, William J. Short (New York: New City Press, 1999), 254.
2. Ibid., 254.
3. Ibid., 255.
4. Ibid., 255.
5. Ibid., 255.
6. Ibid., 255-6.
7. Ibid., 255.
8. Ibid., 256.
9. Ibid., 256–7.
10. Flora Slosson Wuellner, *Miracle: When Christ Touches Our Deepest Hunger* (Nashville: Upper Room Books, 2008), 13.
11. Ibid., 13.
12. Howard Thurman, *Deep Is the Hunger* (New York: Harper & Brothers, 1951), Meditation 203.

Second Week

1. Thomas of Celano, *The Saint*, 256.
2. Ibid., 255.

Third Week

1. Francis of Assisi, *Saint Francis of Assisi: Writing and Early Biographies*, English Omnibus of the Sources for the Life of St. Francis, ed. Marion A. Habig (Quincy, IL: Franciscan Press, 1991), 86.
2. Ibid., 118–19.

3. Ilia Delio, OSF. *The Humility of God: A Franciscan Perspective* (Cincinnati, OH: St. Anthony Messenger Press, 2005), 50–51.
4. Ibid., 56–57. Quoting Thomas of Celano in *The Life of Saint Francis*.
5. Paul Moses, *The Saint and the Sultan: The Crusades, Islam, and Francis of Assisi's Mission of Peace* (New York: Doubleday, 2009), 2.
6. Sr. Mary Jo Chaves, Presentation at Franciscan Spiritual Center, April 2, 2018.

Fourth Week

1. Larry J. Peacock, *Openings: A Daybook of Saints, Psalms, and Prayer* (Woodstock, Vermont: Skylight Paths Publishing, 2014), 375.
2. Francis of Assisi, *Saint Francis of Assisi*, 47.
3. Ibid., 130–31.
4. Ibid., 125–26.

Fifth Week

1. Thomas of Celano, *The Saint*, 40.
2. Andrae Crouch, "Through It All" in *The United Methodist Hymnal* (Nashville, TN: The United Methodist Publishing House, 1989), 507.
3. Gerard Thomas Straub, *The Sun and Moon Over Assisi: A Personal Encounter with Francis and Clare* (Cincinnati, OH: St. Anthony Messenger Press, 2000), 231.
4. Ibid., 196. Taken from a letter from Saint Francis to the faithful.
5. Francis of Assisi, *The Founder*, Francis of Assisi: Early Documents, vol. 2, eds. Regis J. Armstrong, J.A Wayne Hellman, William J. Short (New York: New City Press, 2000), 642.

About the Author

Larry Peacock is director of the Franciscan Spiritual Center in Milwaukie, Oregon. He served as executive director of Rolling Ridge Retreat and Conference Center in North Andover, Massachusetts, for eleven years. A retired United Methodist pastor, Peacock is a trained spiritual director, an author, and a retreat leader.